Bad Birds 2

*Another collection of (mostly) true stories
starring the gobblers
we all love to hate*

By Jim Spencer

Bad Birds 2

Copyright © 2020 by Jim Spencer

Cover photo by Tes Randle Jolly

All rights reserved. No part of this book, either in part or in whole,
may be reproduced, transmitted or utilized in any form or by any means,
electronic, photographic or mechanical, including photocopying, recording, or
by any information storage and retrieval system, without permission in writing
from the publisher, except for brief quotations embodied
in literary articles and reviews.

Requests for permission to make copies of any part
of this book should be made to Treble Hook Unlimited,
P.O. Box 758, Calico Rock, AR 72519

Quantity discounts are available to your company or nonprofit
for reselling, educational purposes, subscription incentives, gifts and
fundraising campaigns. For more information, please contact the publisher.

International Standard Book Number: 978-1-7356117-0-9

To turkey hunters one and all –

to those who succeed,
to those who fail ...

to those who win,
to those who lose ..

to those who have been chasing 'em for decades,
to those who have yet to make that first fateful hunt ...

and especially,
to those who, after getting beat
by still another Bad Bird,
pick themselves up,
dust themselves off,
shake their heads, smile a little,
and march right back into the fray.

Contents

	Dedication	9
	Foreword	11
	Introduction	15
	Prologue	21
1	Gabby	33
2	The Spoil Banks Gobblers	39
3	Han Solo	45
4	The Homebody	49
5	Escort to the Queen	53
6	The Roadrunner	57
7	Marconi	63
8	The Outlaw	67
9	Minnetonka	73
10	Sir Edmund	79
11	Harry S	85
12	Lazybones	91
13	The Bluff Dweller	95
14	Lucky	101
15	Woodrow Too	105
16	She	111
17	Br'er Rabbit	117
18	The Paintball King	123

19	Devil Anse	129
20	Steve Martin	133
21	Ringo	137
22	Blinky	143
23	The Lineman	149
24	The Sundance Kid	153
25	The Sherpa of Matney Mountain	159
26	Parker	165
27	The Gobbler of Heart Attack Mountain	171
28	The Surprise Gobbler	177
29	The Multigobbler	183
30	The Eddiceton Warrior	189
31	The King of the Food Plots	195
32	Jay's Pet	201
33	The Iron Gobbler	207
34	In It to Win It	215
35	All You Have to do is Try	225
36	The Loaner Gun	233
37	The Evolution of a Turkey Hunter	239
38	Hunting on the Shady Side of 70	249
39	Epitaph for a Turkey Hunter	259
40	The Gift Bird	269
	Epilogue	279

Dedication

This one's for Jill.

Hunting partner, writing partner, adventure partner

and life partner, all rolled into one.

You can't beat a deal like that.

Bad Birds 2

Foreword by Ron and Tes Jolly.

Foreword

By Ron and Tes Jolly

Tes and I first met Jim Spencer over 20 years ago on a turkey hunt on Brandywine Island, near Memphis, TN. We were working on a video for Woods Wise Products. Taking a video camera on a turkey hunt is already problem enough, but to further complicate things, we were using muzzle-loading shotguns.

Before the hunt we briefed Jim about the signals we used to communicate what the camera could see and when to pull the trigger. The signals were simple: one kee-kee meant the cameraman had the gobbler in the viewfinder. The second kee-kee was the signal to kill him.

The first afternoon we struck a gobbler and quickly got into position. The gobbler cooperated and closed the distance. I saw Spencer make a slight adjustment to his aim and put his cheek down on the stock of the gun. Seconds passed and I still hadn't seen the gobbler. Spencer made another aim adjustment and still I couldn't find the bird.

Finally, after several minutes with the longbeard in easy range of Spencer's gun, I was able to get bits and pieces of the big tom's backside as he lost interest and faded into the timber. When he was gone Spencer pulled down his mask and grinned at me over his shoulder. "You couldn't see him, could you?"

I shook my head. "You should have killed him anyway," I said.

"Naw," he said, "that wasn't the deal. You couldn't get any footage, so I didn't want to shoot. It's just a turkey."

He never complained, whined or griped. He simply put his head down and gave it his all for the next two days. We never got another chance to tag a bird but Spencer proved to us he is a turkey man.

He's also a pretty decent turkey writer. Before and since that long-ago day, Jim Spencer has written literally hundreds of turkey hunting stories – and, now, three turkey books. He's written a Bad Birds piece for every single issue of Turkey and Turkey Hunting Magazine since Fall 2001. His first Bad Birds book featured over 40 *bad birds*.

Every turkey hunter has met his or her share of *bad birds*. These are the gobblers that always seem to stay one step ahead of us. They get in our heads and cause the loss of sleep, hair, jobs and the occasional marriage.

For years, reading Jim's Bad Birds columns, Tes and I wondered how one man could encounter so many birds that earn the title *bad*? We wondered if our impression of Spencer, formed over 20 years ago on Brandywine Island, was wrong. Then the light bulb came on.

The clarity came from reading his many accounts of *bad bird* duels. Some battles he lost, but others he won. To Spencer, a *bad bird* doesn't have to be one he doesn't kill. A *bad bird* is simply a worthy adversary, a gobbler that doesn't come running in to die. In other words, a bird that makes him work. A bird that makes him think.

The reality is, every turkey gobbler has some *bad bird* in him. The ones that come easy are rarely remembered. It's the hard ones that live in our memories forever.

Jim Spencer hunts turkeys the old-fashioned way. He hunts alone, mostly, on public land, mostly, and covers a lot of ground in the process. He doesn't sit in shooting houses or pop-up blinds, and you could count the times he's used a turkey decoy on your fingers and toes. In short, he is an old school hunter, and when you hunt old school you are going to encounter plenty of *bad birds*. After more than 40 years on the hunt, Spencer is steeped in turkey hunting tradition and turkey hunting wisdom – most of the latter gained the hard way. He plays the game to win but realizes the win is much more than just the kill.

Foreword

Spencer's talent at telling good turkey stories on paper has been honed over a freelance writing career spanning – so far – 60 years. For 20 of those years he was also a writer and editor for the Arkansas Game and Fish Commission. His descriptions of the personalities of the *bad birds* in both this book and the Bad Birds book that preceded it completely explain why these turkeys were bad. And as you read, suddenly you realize you have met a bird just like that. It's what makes the sport of turkey hunting what it is: challenging, exciting and often maddening.

In reality, we all know there is no such thing as a turkey that can't be killed. There are, however, turkeys that can't be killed fair and square, and those are the ones we never forget. Then there are also the ones that require an extra amount of effort and/or dedication, and those are the ones that comprise this book.

But there's more than light-hearted turkey hunting stories here. Do NOT neglect to read the Epilogue. Spencer says it's the most important thing he's *ever* written about turkeys and hunting them, and we don't doubt it. In fact, it may be one of the most important pieces ever written on the turkey hunting subculture. The fact that this old turkey chaser is willing to tackle the gorilla in the room by addressing the current state of wild turkeys and turkey hunting tells you all you need to know about Jim Spencer. He is a turkey man who can spin a tale with the best, but also a turkey man we can all relate to, and in the process open our eyes to the ethics, principles, traditions and lore of our great sport.

Enjoy the read!

Ron and Tes Jolly
Tuskegee, Alabama
August 2020

The rush affects all genders and age groups. Ohio hunters Mekayla and Easton Dye, now teenagers several years older than they were in this picture, still come down with roaring cases of the yips when a gobbler approaches.

Introduction

Dealing With the Rush

We hunt turkeys for many reasons: the challenge of the hunt, the joy of being Out There, the delicious meat – and, of course, the gobble. But the most important reason we hunt them, even more than the gobble, is the adrenaline rush.

Without that rush, this complex, exciting turkey hunting subculture wouldn't exist. But it's there, in spades, and like my old friend and hero Tom Kelly wrote, we are helpless in the grip of our compulsion.

Turkey hunters use adrenaline like Popeye uses spinach, but the chemical surge we so crave often leads us astray. Adrenaline is "fight-or-flight" fuel, and when neither fight nor flight is appropriate, adrenaline gets cranky and creates a feeling of urgency and near-panic. Neither is desirable in turkey hunting; those emotions cause us to over-react, to outrun our headlights, to put ourselves in situations that usually lead to failure. There are many examples of these untenable situations in this book.

One of the most common ways turkey hunters over-react is by closing the distance too rapidly when going to a gobbling turkey. The almost overwhelming urge is to get there *right now*, but fast usually also means noisy. A gobbler can hear leaves crunching farther than you think, and regardless of what you've been told, a man walking does not sound like a turkey walking. Turkeys know this.

Furthermore, there's always the possibility of getting busted. Unless a turkey is gobbling with every breath, you don't have a continuous fix on him. All you know is where he was when he gobbled last, and he might have moved toward you since then. If he's not gobbling pretty much continuously, he can cover a lot of ground between gobbles. If he's a hundred yards closer than you think, you're probably going to bump him.

You don't have to tip-toe around like a cat stalking a robin, but it pays to approach cautiously, being as stealthy as reasonably possible. Vary your walking cadence if you're close and the leaves are crunchy. A turkey doesn't walk at a steady pace. You shouldn't either.

Here's another scenario where over-reaction is the norm: It's midmorning, and as far as you can tell there's nobody gobbling. You're covering ground – prospecting, they call it – and suddenly things break loose. Just over the crest of a nearby ridge, the gobble in response to your crow call nearly knocks you down. He can't be 50 yards away, and your heart rate triples. You panic, you fall down beside the nearest tree, you fumble your facemask on and raise your gun. You yelp at him. He roars back.

The encounter so far has taken 15 seconds, but already you've make two serious mistakes. First, you had enough time to find a better tree than the spindly persimmon you chose, which is not only much too small but is also growing out of a rockpile. The gobbler answered a crow call, and he wasn't likely to come to it. But your panic attack made you sit down wrong, and then, mistake 2, you immediately made a hen call. Now you're stuck. He's very close, very likely coming, and you can only hope he gets there before the fist-sized rocks you sat down on a while ago start punching holes in your ass.

It's simple to avoid falling into traps like this. There's no way to predict when one of those nearby gobbles is going to spin your hat around, but you can be ready when it does by picking out a suitable tree and standing or sitting beside it before calling. Every single time, before you call, do this one simple thing. If one gobbles close you'll still panic, but at least when you fall beside a tree it'll be a good one.

Also, when a gobbler is that close, he probably heard you walking and scuffling around when you sat down. Often that's enough to make him investigate, so wait a few minutes before calling again. This is a good idea whether he gobbled at a crow call or a turkey call, or whether he gobbled on his own and you just happened to be close. At this point, he's not likely to run off. By waiting, sometimes you can "take his temperature," and get some idea of how to call to him. If he's close enough you can hear him drumming, maybe you've already said enough. If he gobbles farther away, you can either reposition or try to call him back.

Another common rush-producing situation is the turkey that gobbles at everything. When he answers every call it increases the adrenaline flow, and the resulting tendency of most hunters is to overcall. Granted, it's thrilling when a bird gobbles 300 times in an hour. But a bird that talky tends to attract attention from other hunters, and anyway, you can't wrap your tag around a bunch of gobbles.

Again, try to control the rush. Don't let it control you. If you're in hilly terrain and can move without being seen, you can often use such a turkey's gabbiness against him. Because he's so vocal, it's easy to keep track of his whereabouts, and you can use that knowledge to get ahead of him if he's moving, or close the gap and get into a good calling position if he's holding still.

Get on the gobbler's level if you can, and get as close as possible without running the risk of bumping him. Sometimes I've been able to get within 30 to 40 yards of talkative gobblers, and when you're that close you're inside what Gary Sefton, in his book *Lessons Learned From the Magnificent Bird*, calls "the must-investigate zone." At this range, often all you need are a few soft purrs and whines to get a gobbler in front of the gun.

That is, a few soft purrs and whines...and patience. It may take him an hour to move the few yards that will make him vulnerable, but if you're that tight on him it will probably happen – if you wait for it, control the rush and don't force the play.

Of course, there's always the possibility of getting *too* close to a gobbling turkey, as we've already mentioned here. This is most likely to happen early in the day, when the turkey is still on the roost. It's also more common early in the season, when the leaves are small or absent and visibility in the woods is much better, and before you remember just how acute a turkey's senses really are.

But in most turkey hunting situations, closer is better. Good hunting strategy dictates that the hunter try to get into the best calling position before the bird flies down, and this usually means getting fairly close. So it's worth the risk, as long as you're careful and don't get stupid.

"The difference between being close enough to a gobbling turkey and being too close is one step," one of my turkey mentors told me long ago. That's true, as far as it goes. But which step is it? The thing to remember is that fatal step does exist. Somewhere between you and that turkey is the Rubicon. If you cross it, you're beat. The challenge is to figure out where that line is and stop just short of it. Ambiguous? Sure. But hey, turkey hunting is an inexact science.

Almost as important as getting in tight on a roosted gobbler is having some idea which direction he's going to fly down. It won't help you to be 80 yards north of a roosted bird if he flies down going south.

Still, if the bird doesn't fly down in your direction, that doesn't mean all is lost. Chapter 4, The Homebody, is a prime example. Don't give up too quick. If the gobbler responded to your call before flying down, he wasn't alarmed, and trust me, he remembers where you are. He just had other ideas at the moment. Before you chase along behind him, try calling him back. Unless he's with hens, it works oftener than you'd think, and anyway, every time you change set-ups, you run the risk of spooking him.

It may take several hours for the gobbler to get back around to you, but it's a pretty good bet that if he answered you from the limb,

Introduction

Spurs like this are why dealing with the rush is so important, but they're also why it's often so difficult.

he'll eventually check you out. My rule of thumb: if I can still hear him gobbling from my original set-up, I'll give him an hour before moving. If he moves closer during that hour, I sit tight. If he doesn't, I'll either follow or look for another contestant, depending on how hot the gobbler seems.

No matter how many precautions you take, though, you're still going to find yourself mired in unfortunate situations of your own making. Such is the power of the rush; such is the nature of turkey hunting. This book (not to mention its predecessors, *Bad Birds 1* and *Turkey Hunting Digest*) wouldn't exist otherwise. Every turkey is different, and every turkey hunt differs from every other turkey hunt. Even the same turkey will react differently on different days. And that's why turkey hunting is at once fascinating and frustrating.

Combine this almost universal unpredictability with the heart-pounding, near-debilitating effects of the rush, and there's no way for mere mortals like us to avoid making mistakes. We can try to minimize those mistakes – and we should – but still they're going to happen.

All of which is as it should be. Turkey hunting is supposed to be tough.

That's the whole point.

Prologue

The Turkey Hunt

Author's note: This piece was Chapter 1 in Turkey Hunting Digest, the award-winning book I wrote back in 2003. It's included here because I think it does a pretty good job of examining the crux of this complicated enterprise we simply call "turkey hunting." My apologies if you've already read it.

(I say that last thing to be polite. Actually, I don't give a damn whether you've read it or not. I think it establishes a solid floor for the book that follows, the way a bass guitar lays down a foundation upon which to build a rock and roll song.)

So here it comes again. Ignore, enjoy or disagree, as you see fit. But don't try to tell me I shouldn't have printed it again, because you'd be wrong.

Sometimes the urge holds off till after New Year's Day. More often, though, it starts pulling at me around Thanksgiving, when our family feasts on the succulent flesh of a wild turkey gobbler, the bird having been saved against this meal from the previous spring's hunting efforts. So far, we haven't had to get our Thanksgiving bird from the supermarket...but once or twice the Christmas bird has come from there.

Regardless of their pedigree, these holiday birds are still turkeys. And wild or tame, they set the cognitive wheels turning. Before the bird is even digested, the familiar fever starts its insidious work. Before day's end, I've retrieved slate calls, diaphragms and my trusty Lohman box with all the notches in its side from the drawers and closets where they've been since late May. Once again, the house, yard and cab of the truck are filled with clucks, purrs, yelps, cackles and cutts – rusty at first, but then sweeter and surer as the old skills and muscle memory resurface.

By the time the last of the inevitable turkey salad is gone, everyone within earshot is tired of the discordant-to-them, lovely-to-me sounds of hen turkeys in love. This, mind, is still November, with spring turkey season nearly four months away.

Non-turkey hunters just don't get it. They can no more make sense of our compulsion than they can understand Chinese hip-hop music. But they're not the only ones; we the afflicted don't understand, either.

And compulsion it most certainly is, as surely as it is compulsion that drives lemmings into the sea or swallows to Capistrano. Tom Kelly admits this in his landmark turkey hunting book *Tenth Legion*: "I do not hunt turkeys because I want to, I hunt them because I have to. I would really rather not do it, but I am helpless in the grip of my compulsion."

But don't misunderstand. Those of us who are thus compelled aren't really complaining. From time to time we may make noises to that effect, especially when the turkey gods are frowning, or when the season is four weeks old and we're deep into sleep deprivation. By and large, though, we've come to accept our lot. For better or worse, we are turkey hunters. And either it gets better…or it gets worse.

Because here's the horrible, hideous truth of it: there is no lukewarm where turkey hunters are concerned. There is no halfway. Either you is or you ain't, and so we is, beset with all the attendant joys and sorrows, highs and lows, pains and pleasures that are part and parcel to this peculiar pastime.

Even among outdoor types, non-turkey hunters outnumber turkey hunters by a wide margin. Judging from the increase in human traffic on both private and public land, that gap may be narrowing, but

Prologue

Here's the horrible, hideous truth of it: there is no halfway in turkey hunting. Either you is or you ain't.

still, it's a good bet that some folks reading these words have no clue what we're talking about here. If you've never personally experienced the rush and roar of turkey hunting, there's no way you can understand it. I know this for a fact, since for the first three decades of my life I didn't have a clue, either. Then I went turkey hunting. And then, as my Pawpaw used to say, I was plumb, slap-dab ruint.

So, go with me on a typical spring turkey hunt. Learn firsthand what this business is all about, and perhaps get ruint yourself:

* * *

Turkey hunters get up *early*. Three o'clock is about right, if you're going to meet me at the crossroads by half past four. No threat implied or intended, but here comes a solemn promise: if you're late, even a minute or two, I'll leave without you. Gobbling turkeys don't wait for tardy turkey hunters, and neither do I.

Lock your truck and ride with me. Yours looks too shiny and new to go where we're heading. Old Blue is used to the rough roads, and looks it. Another ding or two won't even be noticeable. Don't forget any of your gear – shotgun, shells, camouflage, calls, gloves, seat cushion, coffee thermos, water bottle. Just throw it all except the coffee in the back of the truck, on top of my stuff, but hurry up. We're burning precious time, and there are 20 miles of rough road and a considerable hike between us and our bird.

I roosted him late yesterday evening. In turkey hunter's lingo, that means I heard him fly up into a tree for the night and gobble a time or two after he got there. So I already know exactly where he is, and that gives us a little edge on this morning's hunt. But it's only an edge if we get there early enough to take advantage of it. Come on! Let's go!

Okay, while we're driving to get to this turkey, let me tell you a little about what you've gotten yourself into here. A turkey hunt isn't so much a hunt as a military maneuver. If he's gobbling, or if you've roosted him the night before – as we have this one – you already know the bird's location so you're not actually *hunting* him, in the strictest sense of the word. Rather, you're trying to get in a good position and entice him to overcome his inbred reluctance to come to an unseen hen. See, in the real world of turkeydom, a gobbler holds his ground and the hen comes to him. Our goal this morning is to reverse that process and get the gobbler to do the traveling. We're trying to trick him. We're trying to outsmart him.

No, scratch that. I misspoke. You can't outsmart a gobbler, because he isn't smart. He's a bird, after all, with a brain that would rattle around in a ping pong ball. How smart can he be?

What you're trying to do is out-maneuver him, to bend his will to yours, to get him to do something his every instinct is screaming at him not to do. You have to overcome his native caution in order to achieve success, and to do so, you must contend with a set of senses – hearing and eyesight only; thank God they can't smell – so incredibly sharp even veteran turkey hunters are continually amazed. It's been said that a turkey can see through a thin rock, but of course that's ridiculous. What they really do is see *around* them.

Philosophy and semantics aside, we've come here to kill this turkey, and now it's time to leave the truck pinging in the cool morning air and hike through the dark woods to where he slept last night. It's a classic case of good news/bad news: it's not far as the crow flies, but we're not crows. We have two deep valleys and two steep ridges to negotiate, and not much time left to do it. So let's go.

What? You forgot your face mask? Hold still, then, and let me put some of this face paint on you. It's better than a mask, anyway. A face mask restricts your peripheral vision and doesn't do your hearing any good, either. A turkey hunter needs every edge he can get.

We'll be able to use our flashlights for about half the trip, because the bird is roosted on the top of the second ridge and he won't

Contrary to popular belief, turkeys can't see through rocks. Instead, they see around them. Thank God they can't smell; nobody would ever kill one.

be able to see us or hear us until we crest the first one. Before we start, though, put on this orange vest and hat. We'll take off the deer hunting garb when we sit down to work the bird, but it's best to wear it while we're moving, even though it's still dark right now. There'll be some daylight when we get where we're going, and we're not the only hunters in these woods. Not all of them are as careful about target identification as they ought to be.

    Now follow me, and watch your footing. If you step on a loose rock and break an ankle, I'll have to either leave you or quarter you. It would be much too difficult to get you out of here otherwise, and anyway, there's this turkey over there that needs killing.

    I'm joking, of course, but be careful anyway. No sense ruining a hunt by getting hurt before it starts. Let's go.

    What was that you said? We're moving too fast? You need a breather? Hmmm. Listen close: there's a turkey gobbler sleeping in a shortleaf pine two ridges from here. I'm 20 years older than you and 30 pounds heavier, and I'm going to be over there with him when he wakes up. Whether you're there or not is entirely up to you.

Okay. We're past the halfway point and you're still with me. Good on you. We've climbed out of the first valley onto the middle ridge, and it's time to dispense with the flashlights. Some hunters say lights with green lenses won't spook turkeys, but I don't buy it. Dark, that's what doesn't spook turkeys. Don't worry, though. Your eyes will adjust in a few minutes, and there's an old logging trace up ahead that'll take us down this ridge and up the next one pretty close to the turkey.

Here's the road now. It slants down the ridge, following the easiest slopes, and it does the same thing going up the other side. It's fast going and it won't be too hard. Not as hard as the last ridge, anyway. Load your gun now, but do it quietly and don't forget it's loaded. We don't want to make any unnecessary noise once we get in close, but I don't want you shooting yourself and I *really* don't want you shooting me. Be careful, all I'm saying.

We're nearing the top now, and the bird is less than 250 yards away. Keep your voice to a whisper, and don't make any other noise like coughing or farting or breaking sticks underfoot. Remember that sharp hearing I told you about. I wasn't exaggerating.

When we sit down to this turkey, we'll sit against the same tree if we can find one big enough, or against two trees close together if we can't find a big one. You'll be on my left, because you shoot right-handed and I don't, and that way we'll each have our best swing radius to work with. We're getting pretty close to where we need to be now. Don't break any sticks underfoot or I'll twist your neck in a knot.

Okay, that's another joke, but I'm still dead serious about being quiet. Here, this is close enough. Let's sit against this old red oak. It's big enough for both of us, and we'll be able to communicate in low whispers – which I've learned the hard way is highly desirable when you're hunting with a buddy.

The gobbler is roosted slightly down the slope and to the left – your direction – in a small group of big shortleaf pines on the edge of an old clearcut. The cut is too brushy for him to fly down into, so we've got a real good chance of him coming our way. He's 100 yards away now and maybe 25 yards downhill, and there's nothing between us but mature, wide-open woods.

It's a perfect, text-book set-up. I just hope this old boy hasn't read the book.

Take a few seconds to *quietly* rake back the leaves and smooth the ground where you're going to sit. Then take off your orange vest and use it to pad your seat cushion. You need to be as comfortable as possible, because we might have to be as motionless as this tree we're leaning against, and we might have to be that way for a long time. That's hard enough to do even when your ass doesn't hurt.

After you're sitting down, get your knees up and rest the gun across them, to make sure that's going to be a comfortable position when the time comes. Got a rock under where your right foot wants to rest, you say? Okay, that's why you tried it now. You've got time to dig it up and move it out of the way. But do it q-u-i-e-t-l-y.

Okay, we can relax and enjoy the coming of the day…and we didn't get here a minute too soon. There's already a glow in the east, and while the cardinals haven't started yet, I expect they're clearing their throats. The turkeys start gobbling not long after the cardinals start singing. That is, if they gobble at all.

There's the first cardinal. Their song even sounds red, have you ever noticed? He ought to gobble any minute. Maybe I ought to hoot like a barred owl…

Hooooo-awwwww!

Ah, good. My owling's not all that great, but that real owl did the honors for me.

Hooooo-awwwww!

Gobble, will you? What's the matter with him, anyway? Please gobble.

There he is! He's right where I left him last night, and that's never a sure thing. I've had lots of roosted birds move on me during the night, and I don't know why. But I know they sometimes do it, so I'm always a little nervous at first.

We'll let him sound off a few more times, if he will, and then we'll give him a tree yelp or two. Real soft stuff, barely audible to our ears, but he'll hear it just fine. We want to make him think there's a sleepy hen over here who's just waking up.

He's gobbling pretty good now, isn't he? I could sit here and listen to him all day, but he's not going to sit up there that long, and there's work to be done. I like the slate best for this soft stuff. Here goes. Cross your fingers, I'm not very good at tree yelps…

Good. That sounded good. The turkey seemed to think so, too. Did you hear how he walked all over me as soon as I made the first peep? We'll let him gobble once more on his own, and I'll call to him one more time, and then we'll shut up until he flies down. He knows where we are, and there's no sense in overplaying our hand. Calling too much tends to make a turkey gobble too much, and on public land that often attracts other hunters. We don't want that. Calling to a roosted gobbler also tends to make him stay longer in the tree, waiting for the eager hen to come walking underneath him. We don't want that, either. We want him to think there's a hen over here, but leave him with the impression she's not very interested.

There he is again. Now, two or three more soft notes and we're set.

Boy, he gobbled back fast at that series, even though that first yelp was a little sour. We've got his attention, so now we wait him out…

There! Did you hear him fly down? That was a long 15 minutes, wasn't it? I bet he gobbled 50 times, and it was a strain not to call to him some more. But now he's down here with us, and it's time to call to him a little more. I'm gonna yelp at him a little and see what happens.

You be ready. He might come running, or it might take him two hours to cover this 100 yards. Then again, he's just as likely to go the other way, or just stand there and gobble like his foot is nailed to the ground. With a turkey, you never know.

Ah, that's what I was hoping for. He gobbled back before I even finished the yelp. In turkey hunting parlance, that's known as "cutting your call", and it's a very good omen. We might get a look at this bird.

Oooooh, boy, I can hear him drumming. Listen hard; it sounds like a log truck a long way off, right out at the limit of hearing, pulling a hill in granny low. I have friends who can hear the sound at several hundred yards, but 50-odd years of duck hunting have done unpleasant things to my old ears. When I can hear drumming, the turkey is just about shootable. Keep your eyes…

Whoa, there he is! Don't move. He's about 75 yards out, just to the left of that double-trunk dogwood about 45 degrees to the right of your gun barrel. He's strutting, and he's getting a little closer, but he's not in any hurry. Don't move.

All right. Fifty yards now. You see him, don't you? Good. Getting to watch the show is the best part of the hunt. Look at him, blown up as big as a Russian boar and just as black. Wait until he goes behind that white oak, then shift your gun around.

Good. He didn't see the movement. If we don't screw things up, you're about to kill this turkey. Keep the gun on him as he comes, but make sure you're slow and deliberate with it. No jerky moves.

Let him come on at least until he's even with that stump. It's about 40 yards, and that'll put him in range. If he wants to come closer, let him. Thirty yards would be better. If he gobbles, try not to flinch. It'll be loud at this range, and I can tell by your breathing you've already got a pretty good case of the yips. Don't be embarrassed; so have I.

He's even with the stump now, but he's still coming so let him. Lordy, isn't he something! Look at that beard, thick as a bell rope. I bet he weighs 22 pounds. You've done everything right so far, so just stay

Prologue

Be ready. I'm gonna let him come another yard or so, and then…

as calm as you can and think things through. Don't blow it by making a mistake at this late stage of the game, the way I've done so many times.

Let him come. Let him come…

Thirty yards now, more or less. Don't shoot him while he's strutting; his skull and neck are pulled down into his chest and they present a smaller target now. Also, you're liable to shoot most of his beard off. Make sure, *make sure,* your cheek is down on the stock and you're looking straight down the gun barrel. If your head's not down you'll shoot over him sure as death and taxes.

Be ready. I'm gonna let him come another yard or so, and then I'll cluck at him pretty loud. That ought to make him break strut and stretch his neck to take a look, and that's when you need to shoot him. You'll have a second or two to get it done, so don't rush it. But don't dawdle, either, because he won't stay stretched out like that forever.

Aim at the base of his wattles, where things are biggest and

reddest. That'll put the upper part of your pattern in his neck and head. *And keep your head down on that gun.*
　　Ready? Here we go. Show time.
　　Cluck!

1

Gabby

Camp Robinson Wildlife Management Area in central Arkansas is a mix of hogback granite ridges, thickets, swampy creek bottoms, hardwood flats, pine plantations, old fields and natural prairie, with a cypress-tupelo swamp thrown in for good measure. It's a National Guard training facility, but 25,000 of its 40,000 acres are wild and uninhabited. The diverse habitat makes for a thriving turkey population, and the 50 to 100 permits issued each spring (back then) were eagerly sought by local hunters. In the mid-1990s, I was lucky enough to draw a permit in two consecutive years, and I spent both of those three-day hunts trying to get the drop on one particular gobbler I named Gabby.

The 200 or so acres Gabby called home had a little of almost everything Camp Robinson had to offer. Two long, narrow pine plantations ran east and west, separated by a low, boggy hardwood flat about a hundred yards wide and 600 yards long. A spring run creek with mossy rocks meandered through the hardwoods. In the middle of the flat were several randomly-spaced humps of granite, little mini-ridges that didn't amount to much but broke up the flat relief of the hardwoods. Outside each pine plantation was a brushy strip of honeysuckle, sumac and smilax, and the brush played out on the south into a wide field of bluestem prairie.

It was an ideal place for a dominant gobbler to set up shop, and Gabby was a dominant gobbler. The only downside was that the place was too handy; a pair of well-maintained and well-traveled gravel

The 200 or so acres Gabby called home had everything a dominant gobbler needed, including a spring creek for a permanent water supply.

roads formed its north and east boundaries.

Since Gabby was a noisy turkey (hence his name,) everybody and his brother knew about him. All you had to do to hear him was stop on either road just about any morning during March or April. I remember one warm pre-season morning when five of us stood on the north road, listening to Gabby rack 'em off one after another from his position in the hardwood flat, barely 80 yards from where we all stood grinning at one another. He must've gobbled a hundred times in the 15 minutes I was there.

On the first day of the first year's three-day hunt, three vehicles were parked on the two gravel roads that bounded Gabby's stomping ground. I went elsewhere, but when I came back through at 9 a.m. after getting beaten by another gobbler, all three vehicles were gone. I figured Gabby was, too, but I heard him gobble while I was still getting my bullet launcher out of the truck. He was out there in the hardwood flat, right where he was supposed to be.

Three hours later he was still there, despite my best efforts. He'd slowed down some, but was still gobbling a dozen times an hour when I quit him.

The second day there were two vehicles at Gabby's house, and they were gone when I checked back at mid-morning after getting beat elsewhere. Before-work hunters, I surmised. Or maybe just candy-asses. Whichever, Gabby was still talking, and again he refused to come in. I gave him four hours this time. In the seven hours I'd hunted him, Gabby had stayed in the hardwood flat, moving seemingly at random but never leaving the protective open woods of the flat. I saw him three times. He was a good bird and I wanted him badly.

The third morning I got there early, and was the first vehicle to park. I was still walking through the pines toward the hardwood flat, though, when two other vehicles pulled up and stopped on the gravel. I heard truck doors open and close, and voices. I said a couple things my mother didn't teach me, walked back to my truck, and at 9 came back to find the other guys gone. Gabby was still there, still gobbling, still refusing to leave the hardwoods. I gave him another three hours of my life and went home to make turkey tag soup.

After drawing another permit the next year, I found Gabby still in apparently sole possession of the hardwood flat. I spent a couple hours five mornings during the week before the hunt trying to pattern this maddening turkey, but the only pattern I could find didn't help much: he stayed in the hardwood strip, where it was so open and the tree trunks so skinny a good set-up was nearly impossible. But the first morning I was on him anyway, getting in there so early I had to wait an hour in total darkness. This time no one came in on top of me, and when Gabby started yodeling at first light, I was the only one there to hear him.

I was sitting at the edge of the north pine plantation, at the narrowest part of the hardwood strip. It was still 75 yards wide, but Gabby's habit was to stay right in the middle of the strip, and that would put him less than 40 yards off the gun barrel. If he came by me he'd be in trouble.

But that morning Gabby broke pattern. For the first time since I'd met him, he entered the south pines and circled my position, coming back out into the hardwoods once he was well out of range. I fooled with him all morning, changing positions a half-dozen times. I saw him twice, but he never came closer than 80 yards.

The next morning, I went into the middle of the hardwood strip and set up against a 12-inch post oak, the biggest tree I could find. Gabby came straight at me but stopped at 50 yards, eyeballed the suspicious-looking blob at the foot of the post oak, and turned around. He spent the rest of the morning in the east half of the hardwood strip, often visible but never anywhere close to gun range.

On the last morning, I again came early. Again I was alone to hear him gobble at first light. But this time I was laying flat on my belly atop one of the granite humps that poked out of the hardwood flat. I'd avoided them before because there weren't any trees on them and they consisted entirely of uncomfortable chunk rock and blackberry canes, but I'd given this turkey five days of my hunting career and was pretty sure I'd never have another chance at him. I figured a little discomfort was in order.

If I'd done that the first day, I'd never have considered him a Bad Bird. He gobbled a lot on the roost, flew down and kept it up. He headed my way at my first run of yelps. Seventeen minutes after his feet touched the ground I was standing on his neck.

2

The Spoil Banks Gobblers

The place was a scabbed-over strip mine. Mined and abandoned a hundred years ago, the 1300-odd acre public area had the topography of a wrinkled piece of old corduroy. The dirt they'd removed to get at the coal had been left in irregular rows, and it had haired over with a hodgepodge of hardwoods – hackberry, elm, cherry, bois d'arc, locust, with oaks and hickories beginning to show up here and there.

The ridges ran more or less north and south, but you couldn't depend on it. Every once in a while a cross-ridge would mess up the landscape's rough symmetry. And then, as if getting around in there wasn't already tough enough, there was an interconnecting network of deeper furrows, now canals, that had apparently provided some sort of system for getting the coal out of the mined area. These canals were 40 to 100 feet wide, deep enough to float a river barge, and it seemed like you couldn't go 300 yards in any direction without running into one.

Those spoil bank ridges weren't tall. Thirty to 40 feet on average, I'd say, with an occasional hump soaring to 50 or 60 feet. But they were steep as the Alps, and usually their tops were sharp as the roof of an A-frame house. The dirt was poor so the timber was junk, thickety and low, with taller trees occasionally poking through what otherwise was a 25-foot canopy. Throw in the minor fact that many of the valleys between ridges held long, narrow puddles of tannin-stained water from four inches to four feet deep, and what you had was one hellish place to hunt.

But there were turkeys in it, and that was my doom.

The place had either been given to or had been bought by the state and was now a wildlife management area, and I'd found it by doing some map-scouting. I'd never been on the ground there, and went in blind the first day without knowing it was an old strip mine.

It didn't take me long to figure it out, though. And I'd have left immediately, except that I could hear no less than six gobblers greeting the day out there in the wrinkled landscape. On my most resolute day, I've never been able to turn my back on a half-dozen talkative gobblers. So I soon found myself clawing my way up and down those spoil piles, fighting thickets and vines, working my way around or through the puddles in the valleys, trying to get shapes on one – any one – of those gobblers.

I busted turkeys out of trees. I topped spoil piles and busted turkeys off the ground. I walked past turkeys that were gobbling too infrequently for me to keep track of them. Finally, after blundering around in that hideous place for the better part of the morning, I got on a bird and thought I had him coming to the call.

I did, too, but I'd misjudged things and when he showed up he was two spoil banks over from my position. I could catch an occasional glimpse of him over there, strutting along the knife-edge of his bank, but he wouldn't cross the two valleys between his position and mine. He was just out of range, and eventually the encounter fizzled out.

I fully intended to hunt somewhere else – anywhere else – the following day, but the memory of all those gobblers pulled at me all night. The second morning found me back on the area, but this time at the south side rather than the east side. My reasoning was that I'd be able to travel along the length of the spoil banks rather than having to cross them at right angles. My reasoning was correct but it didn't help much. The banks were so steep and narrow on top that it was like side-hilling a ski jump. If one leg had been 18 inches shorter than the other, I might have made it okay. But my legs are pretty much the same length, which left me woefully ill-equipped.

But the turkeys were just as plentiful and just as talky as they'd been the day before, and as near as I could tell I heard an even dozen gobblers that day. I had an exciting but frustrating morning pursuing and working first one of them and then another, five turkeys in all, but in one way or another, every one of them flummoxed me. Two were repeats of the day before: they came in but they were two spoil banks over, visible but out of gun range. Two others gobbled and moved all around one side of me, but wouldn't come – apparently because there were too many landscape wrinkles between us. One came in on my ridge, but stayed too far out in the brushy woods for me to shoot him. He hung up at about 60 yards, gobbling and drumming, and when time ran out for the day he was still nailed down. I left him gobbling.

Day three was my last chance to hunt in that part of the world, and as much as I wanted to go elsewhere, I just wasn't strong enough to do it. But this final morning, I went to the west boundary of the area, where the strip mines bordered an expanse of shaggy pasture on private land. An old access road ran along the fence, just inside the public boundary, and I stayed on it as I moved slowly north along the boundary line, watching the open field ahead.

As careful as I was, though, the gobbler that was out there saw me before I saw him. When I picked him out in the broom 200 yards ahead, he was already in sneak-out-of-there mode. Having no other options, I stopped in my tracks and let him do it. Thinking he was still undetected, the bird sneaked from clump to clump of the long grass, standing still and watching me for seconds at a time between moves, while I watched him out of the corner of my eye and pretended I didn't see him. Finally he crossed the fence and disappeared, into the public land and into the spoil banks.

I gave him 20 minutes, then eased up to where I'd seen him go in. Here, the ridges ran east and west, and I figured he'd gone in a ways and was cooling his heels until returning to the open field. I climbed one of the ridges, eased in carefully for 75 yards or so, and sat down to wait.

Twenty minutes later, he gobbled, no more than 200 yards from me and either on the ridge I was on or the one next to it. I yelped three times, soft, and he gobbled back.

Easy does it, I coached myself. *Don't screw this up.* Following my own counsel, I never made another call until I clucked to get him to raise his head for the shot. I'd had him in sight for 15 minutes as he moved slowly along the crest of the next ridge, sneaking back toward the field but also hoping to pick up the hen along the way. When I shot him, he went topknot over teakettle down the back side of the spoil bank and it took me nearly five minutes to fight my way over there to him.

He was a very good turkey, but I'll never hunt that hellhole again.

He was a very good turkey, and I'll remember him and his kinfolk for the rest of my life. But if I ever hunt in that hellhole again, it will be because somebody is holding a gun to my head.

Bad Birds 2

3

Han Solo

To the best of my knowledge, he never gobbled more than once each morning. Hence his monicker: Solo, because he only gobbled the once. Han, because of Harrison Ford's character in the original Star Wars, who was unpredictable in the extreme and also, evidently, pretty much unkillable. Like this turkey. Sorry, but that's the loopy way my brain works.

Han lived in and around a 50-acre pasture that cornered into a big, hard-to-reach section of national forest land. It was hard to reach across the public land, that is. To get there through the public, you had to first drive about two miles along a bumpy, washed-out, half-forgotten two-track, walk one more mile along the two-track after it got too rough to drive, bushwhack through a quarter-mile of brambly, brushy clearcut, then fall off the side of a mountain and lose 700 feet of altitude through a boulder field.

That rough approach pretty much sealed him off from public access. However, if you were on good terms with the lady who owned the pasture, you could get there the easy way – by driving along a smooth private farm lane to the east edge of the pasture, parking at the cattle guard, and walking 600 yards across mostly level ground to the corner where the pasture met the public land.

I was on good terms with the lady, so I was able to get to Han the easy way. But that was the only thing I ever found easy about dealing with him.

I found him the old-fashioned way, through the fruits of pre-season scouting. Standing on a small finger ridge on the private land four days before the season, I heard his single daily gobble at first light. I didn't know at the time he wasn't going to gobble any more, so I listened in vain to hear him again. By the time it became obvious he wasn't going to do it and I started his way, he was already on the ground in the pasture. I sneaked to the edge of the woods and watched him strutting for a while, then backed out.

The next three mornings I was closer to him at first light, and determined from his single gobble each morning that he roosted in a cluster of big shortleaf pines 75 yards off the corner of the field. Okay, fine, but the problem was, he flew down differently each of the three days. Once he sailed into the pasture. Once he pitched out along the slope of the hill and landed 200 yards east of his roost trees. Once, as near as I could tell, he simply fell off his limb and landed beneath the tree.

Han's inconsistency might not have been much of an issue if he'd been more vocal and therefore easier to keep up with. But he wasn't, and I suspected his stinginess with his gobbles was going to give me problems. But turkeys were scarce in my neck of the woods that spring, and I didn't have any other hot prospects. Opening day found me set up at the corner of the pasture.

His single morning gobble came on cue, and for the first time since I'd found him, I answered him with a soft tree call, hoping he'd gobble another time or two. He didn't, but I was close enough to hear him drumming in the tree.

I never saw him until he flew out. This time he exercised a fourth fly-down option by pitching toward the uphill slope and hitting the ground pretty much level with the limb he'd been sleeping on. I picked him up when he left the branch and watched him all the way to the ground, and when he touched down he was already in strut. I made a soft run of yelps, and he turned to face me and started zig-zagging down the slope in my direction.

All right, I thought, *this isn't going to be as tough as I figured.*

Han Solo

Wrong. Han came back about to the base of his roost tree, still 75 yards from me, and changed direction. In full sight in the open woods but twice too far away to shoot, he went past me and into the pasture, where he fooled around for a while before moving on into the woods on the north. I gave him a while and went after him, but couldn't locate him again.

I got in there early enough the second morning of the season to get above him on the slope, so of course this time he left the roost going downhill. He landed within easy shotgun range of the tree I'd been sitting by the day before. Today he waited until he was on the ground before uttering his single daily gobble, and when he did it I hit him hard with a raucous, insistent series of cutting.

Bad move. Han folded his tent, stalked out into the middle of the pasture, and stayed there for two hours while I watched him, wishing all the while I had a rifle. Again he left the field going north, passing under the fence at the same spot as the day before.

Aha, I thought. *I do believe I detect a pattern.*

Wrong again. The third morning found me waiting on the north side of the pasture within shotgun range of where he'd crossed the fence, and I waited there until vines started growing up my legs. Han gave his customary single morning salute shortly after first light, so I know he roosted in those same shortleaf pines. But I was too far away to know what he did after that. All I know is he never came into the pasture that morning.

For all I know, he stayed in the tree all day, because that's where he was on Day Four. I was back near the field corner again, and he gobbled his one time, pitched out uphill, and marched resolutely up the mountain and out of sight.

I'm stubborn, but I try not to be stupid about it. I'd been to this turkey eight days straight, and he had yet to repeat himself. Reasoning that life was short and turkey seasons were shorter, I gave up on Han and went elsewhere, located a more biddable gobbler and tagged him, then called up a bird for a friend the day after that. After a few days, with the pressure now off, I returned to the pasture to give old Mr. Solo one more morning of my dwindling allotment.

He wasn't there. Or, if he was, he'd decided one gobble a day was one too many. At any rate, I didn't hear him or see him that day. More than a week later, after a trip out of state, I went to him again. Again, I didn't hear him. I went back the next day, failed to hear him again, and gave up. Maybe somebody else killed him. Maybe he moved.

Maybe he died of a heart attack, I don't know. The whole encounter ended, as many do, with a question mark instead of an exclamation point. I've taken several other gobblers in the years since in and around that 50-acre pasture, but they were "normal" birds. That is, they gobbled some, and acted predictably some, and in general played their parts in ways that allowed me to play mine.

And every time I've slung one of those birds over my shoulder, I've wondered if maybe it was Han Solo. But I'm pretty sure none of them were. They all gobbled more than once.

The author has killed several gobblers in the vicinity of Han Solo's old stomping grounds. Was one of them Han himself? Probably not.

4

The Homebody

Andy and Dale found him on a Monday. They'd both killed turkeys that morning, and were poking around prospecting for the next day's hunt. They stopped at a well-used parking area on a chunk of public land, and when Dale ran a series of yelps through his slate, the turkey nearly blew their hats off from a patch of thick woods, less than a hundred yards from the truck. Andy left me a text message: "Found you a killable turkey if you can get here quick."

Jill and I got the message after an unproductive morning and I called Andy immediately. They told us where to meet them, and at noon they took us to the spot. With less than 45 minutes left before Missouri's closing bell, we went in and set up. The bird gobbled once at Jill's box call, fairly close, but that was at 12:45 and he hadn't said anything else when shooting hours closed 15 minutes later.

Dale and Andy put him to bed that evening, not 150 yards from that parking area, and hunted him Tuesday. He started gobbling early, and they were able to get in close. So close, in fact, they could see the gobbler in the tree. They watched him stay up there, gobbling about every 45 seconds, until 7:30 a.m. He finally flew down, gobbled several times on the ground 75 yards away, and that's when Dale made his first call of the morning.

It was the last they heard from the gobbler that day. When they finally got up to go elsewhere at 10 o'clock, he hadn't made another peep.

Dale and Andy left for home that afternoon, but Jill and I

stayed. We roosted the gobbler again that afternoon, 100 yards or so from the parking place. But another vehicle was already there when we arrived Wednesday morning, so we went elsewhere. When we drove by the place later in the morning, the parking area was empty. We stopped and I checked him with my old Lohman box. He gobbled right back, not 200 yards away. We gathered our gear and snuck into the woods, and for the next two hours we had a desultory, mostly one-sided conversation with the gobbler. He'd answer occasionally, or gobble on his own, usually about once every 15 minutes. But if he was interested in coming to the call he disguised it well. For the second time, we got up and left his five-acre stomping ground when shooting time expired at 1 p.m.

That evening, we drove to the now-familiar parking area at sundown. He gobbled angrily at my first hoot. He was just where we expected him to be – about 150 yards into the woods, where the flat land started sloping off toward the river.

Well before daylight Thursday morning, we were standing pretty close to where we thought he'd been when he gobbled the previous evening. Sure enough, when he started gobbling at the first hint of dawn, he was less than 75 yards away. We carefully cut the distance by 20 yards and set up, and for the next 90 minutes we listened to him sit in the tree and gobble – 103 times, unless I flubbed the count. Every once in a while I could pick him out in the thick vegetation when he'd run his neck out, but most of the time it was an audio performance only, frequent gobbling and nonstop drumming. He sat up there and gobbled for 90 minutes, and I guess he'd have kept it up for a while longer except that at 7:15 something spooked him. He quit gobbling and started clucking and putting, kept it up for about five minutes, then abruptly flew out of his tree and disappeared, flying south, flying hard. Fox or bobcat, maybe. We never did figure it out.

Five days later, after a highly successful journey to Kansas, we came back. At sundown we drove to the parking area, stopped and

The Homebody

hooted. Right on cue, the turkey gobbled from a tree in the thick woods, less than 150 yards from the parking area.

Jill didn't want anything more to do with this gobbler, but she agreed to drop me off there the next morning before going off to look for a more reasonable bird. When he started gobbling, again in the barest glimmer of the new dawn, I was already close. But I eased in a little closer, stopping this time at about 60 yards. Not quite in sight, but almost.

As was his custom, he stayed in the tree well past normal flydown time. He gobbled 60 times before 7 a.m. and then abruptly shut up. I was beginning to think he'd flown down and left when, at 7:25, he started gobbling again. He sounded off ten more times in the next five minutes and shut up again. Determined to give him my best shot, I just sat tight. So far I hadn't made a call. At 7:55, he gobbled once more, still in the tree. Two minutes later he gobbled again and he was

Andy had told me he thought the gobbler had a thick, bushy beard. He was right.

on the ground, farther away than he'd been in the tree, but still fairly close – 100 yards or so.

I clucked and purred a couple times on a slate, and when he gobbled again two minutes later he was closer. I kept mum. Two more gobbles and he was there, looking for the timid hen, coming through the thick woods in that jerky-headed way turkeys have.

Andy had told me he thought the gobbler had a thick, bushy beard, judging from what he'd seen of it the week before. The old bird was still riding the invisible bicycle to nowhere when I called Andy and told him he was right.

5

Escort to the Queen

The off-colored hen showed up in a long, narrow hayfield that ran for two miles along the river. I first saw her in July, in a mixed flock of hens and poults. She was one of the poults. We continued to see her off and on through that summer, fall and winter when we were fishing, squirrel hunting, trapping or just boondocking. Not frequently, but often enough to more or less keep tabs on her. She'd be on the river, somewhere in the long field, or on the big wooded bluff that bordered the west side of the field.

She wasn't white, but rather a muted silver, and I suppose it was her color that allowed us to glimpse her as often as we did. In good light, if she was close enough, you could see darker markings on her breast and back. Probably the darker feather tips, but I'm guessing about that. Whatever, she was a distinctive, attractive turkey, and from a distance, she stood out like a lantern in a coal mine.

In February, as expected, the local gobblers got a lot more interested in the silver hen and her sisters, and a pod of four longbeards and three jakes started hanging around. The big boys strutted and the jakes gawked from the sidelines, and as February melted into March, the four longbeards went through their sorting-out process.

One bird emerged as the clear boss. He was a magnificent tom, easily identifiable because he was the only one of the four who'd strut unmolested by the others. The other three longbeards would strut, sure, but every time, the boss would sidle over to the strutter, making him slick down and scuttle away.

All through early March I watched him bully his buddies

and court the hens, and almost always the silver one was present. It seemed to me he paid more attention to her than to the others, but that was probably a false impression, caused by the fact that I was always conscious of her presence. Somewhere about that time, I started thinking of her as the "Queen," and the big tom as her Escort.

In mid-March we left the state for an early-season turkey safari to Florida, Alabama and Mississippi. By the time we returned in early April, things had changed. The three subordinate longbeards and two of the jakes were absent, but the flock of hens had grown by six. The Queen was still there, shining like a new dime, and the Escort continued to pay her homage.

I hunted him the first three days of the season. All three days, he spent almost all his time in the south half of the long field. Truth be told, it made for pretty boring hunting. He'd gobble some, but not a lot, and the hens obviously weren't inclined to bring their man over and share him with a hussy who hid in the woods and made such unseemly advances. I am not a decoy fan, but I tried them the second and third days. Didn't make any difference.

The only thing that made those three days more than marginally entertaining was the single remaining jake. He wouldn't do anything when the Escort was gobbling, but when the big boy strutted, the jake got all herky-jerky and walked around going *"YAWK, Yawk, yawk."* I'd heard and seen jakes do that before, but never with such regularity. I think he was reacting to the big bird's drumming, but who knows?

The jake's antics weren't enough to keep me there indefinitely, so I gave up on the Escort for a while. After four or five days of hunting elsewhere, with one tag filled and the second burning a hole in my pocket, I went back to challenge the Escort again…

…and found no turkeys in the field. But I did hear one gobbling on the ridge above it, and when he was quiet, that telltale *"YAWK, Yawk, yawk"* gave me a clue as to who was doing the gobbling.

The ridgetop had a lot of open, flat places where a gobbler could show off, but it was also broken up enough on top with chunk rock, brush, logs and such to allow a careful hunter to move around without being seen. I got in pretty tight and set up, and when I made my first call, the Escort cut me off.

That's when I made my first mistake. I moved on him, in what I thought was a flanking maneuver. But while I was flanking him, he was coming to me. When I made my new set, figuring I'd be right beside him, and clucked to get his attention, he gobbled from the precise spot I'd just vacated.

Nobody ever accused me of being a quick study, so I promptly made mistake number two. I moved again. When I clucked from set three, he immediately gobbled from set two.

Okay. If he wanted to play that game, I could wait. I yelped again, he gobbled again, and I got my gun on my knee. He never gobbled again, but every couple minutes I could hear the blabbermouth jake going *YAWK-Yawk-yawk,* and it didn't seem to be getting any closer. Matter of fact, the sound was fading away, and by the time I realized it and decided to move, the ridge was as innocent of turkeys as the boreal forests of Siberia.

I couldn't hunt the next day, but the day after that I was back on the ridge, listening for the Escort and his squire. I picked them up right off the roost, again in the woods. I let him gobble for a while to see if he had any particular direction in mind, and when he started south along the side of the ridge bordering the field, I hot-footed it in a big circle and set up ahead of him. He came, but not close enough. The Queen and four other hens were with him, and they pulled him wide and I couldn't bend his route enough to get him in range. He and the squire went by at 50 yards, him strutting and drumming and the jake *YAWK-Yawk-yawk*ing, and when I tried to get in front of them again I guessed wrong and never saw or heard them again that day.

The next day I didn't hear any gobbling, but the jake was singing his irritating song farther down the ridge and I homed in on it. I set up 200 yards away from the sound, on a likely travel lane, and never called.

Bad Birds 2

The yawking got closer and closer, and pretty soon the jake came into view. Close behind him was the Escort to the Queen, but the Queen herself wasn't with him. Finally, the Escort was vulnerable.

Three minutes later I was standing over a mighty big gobbler.

At 90 yards he stopped to strut in an open spot on the ridge, and when he hadn't moved in ten minutes, I gave the softest cluck I could manage. He immediately gobbled, then tucked into a muscular, businesslike strut, posing for the unseen hen like one of those buff, oily, steroid-infused guys you see on the covers of body-builder magazines. The jake went *yawk*, and they both started moving in my direction.

Three minutes later I was standing over a mighty big gobbler, and we never saw the Queen again.

6

The Roadrunner

You could count on the Roadrunner. He was a very findable turkey. Killable, though? Not so much.

He was almost always within hearing range of a seldom-used Forest Service road that zig-zagged down the south slope of a huge ridge in the Ouachita Mountains. More than once I saw him in that road, which is how he got his name. He'd usually gobble, and he'd sometimes come, but never all the way.

He was a tough bird to hunt, and several things contributed to the degree of difficulty. One was the variation in altitude of his home range. The Ouachitas aren't the Rockies, but this little mountain system in the heart of fly-over country has its moments. The Roadrunner's home territory ran from an elevation of about 1400 feet to well past 2200 feet. That doesn't sound like much, 800 feet or so. But try climbing that far – or descending that far, which is almost as taxing – in the half-light of dawn, when you're trying to get to a gobbler before he shuts up.

Another factor was the steep terrain. Okay, most of it wasn't a 45-degree slope, but it was steep enough that when you climbed it you had to use your arms as well as your legs, and when you went downhill, it was difficult not to break into a trot. Side-hilling, you had to be always on guard against toppling over. Adding another twist (yes, pun intended,) the deep leaf litter on much of the slope hid a treacherous jumble of ankle-turning rocks from baseball to peach basket size, with a scattering of boulders as big as school buses just to make it interesting.

Then there was the fact that the zig-zag road crossed and

recrossed the Arkansas/Oklahoma border four times as it descended the steep slope. The Roadrunner's home range straddled the line, and back then I couldn't afford nonresident licenses. So whenever I found him gobbling in the Choctaw Nation, I was out of the game.

But the main thing that made him difficult was the fact that he was a Bad Bird, and I think he'd have been just as hard to kill on flat ground. He didn't live on flat ground, though, so if I wanted to hunt him, I had to do it on the steep, bouldery side of this damn mountain. I could have not hunted him, I suppose, but where's the fun in that?

The first time I met the Roadrunner was after a friend heard him gobbling far below, as he sat in his truck beside the road on top of the mountain. "He was gobbling a lot this morning," Ron told me, making an X on my topo map. "But I've been down there before, and that stuff is way too rough for my taste. You can have him. I'll find one somewhere else."

I'd driven that zig-zag road a time or two, but had never hunted there. I was young and bulletproof in those days, though, and figured I was up to the challenge. But that was before the morning the Roadrunner pulled me, not once but three times, up and down most of the 800-odd vertical feet of his home range. Twice during that four-hour torture session I had him close enough to kill, but it never worked out. The first time he hid behind one of those infernal school bus rocks, and the second time I was puffing and blowing so hard after climbing up to him I think he heard me and got spooky. Whatever the real truth, he disappeared, and I couldn't raise him again that morning.

I had to go back to work the next day, but the following Saturday I returned to the zig-zag road. I located him in short order. But he was in Indian territory that day, and try as I might, I couldn't pull him onto legal ground. He flirted with me all morning, though, and I didn't have the willpower to abandon him and go look for another gobbler.

Saturday afternoon he started gobbling about 3:30, and when I got in tight on him I could see him strutting in the zig-zag road, smack-

The Roadrunner

The Roadrunner was a very findable turkey. Not so killable, though.

dab on the state line. It might as well have been the California-Nevada line as the Arkansas-Oklahoma one, though, for all the inclination he showed to investigate my calling. He'd gobble at me but steadfastly refused to come, and I couldn't get any closer than 200 yards because of the dry leaves and the open woods along the road. All I could do was sit there and beg, and evidently he wasn't in a charitable frame of mind.

Sunday morning he was back in Arkansas, roosted on the slope above the road where he'd strutted the afternoon before. I set up barely east of the state line, far enough off the Forest Service road to be legal, and gave him a tree yelp at what I judged to be fly-down time. He'd been gobbling like a barnyard bird until that moment, but after I called he didn't make another peep for almost an hour. When he did, he was 300 feet higher up the mountain and a quarter-mile farther into Arkansas, and even though he gobbled a few times after that, he was traveling and wouldn't let me catch up. I finally gave up at 11 a.m., sweaty and ankle-sore from fighting the rocks and the cow-face slope.

I had the next day off from work, so I stayed over for one more try. I couldn't find him Sunday afternoon, but I did find a secondary road along the contour of the mountain that was lousy with gobbler tracks and other turkey sign. I figured it was as good a place as any to start the Monday morning hunt.

I figured wrong. The Roadrunner was roosted far up the slope. I was about halfway to him when he flew down, pitching downhill toward me and landing almost within gun range. He caught me off guard, and all I could do was stand there teetering on the steep slope and trying to hide behind a skinny dogwood while he pulled himself together after his controlled crash-landing. With nothing between us but 75 yards of air and a spindly tree trunk, I was afraid to call. He puttered around for a few minutes, then let out a ferocious gobble. A hen yelped down there near the secondary road – the one I'd just left – and he headed that way. His route brought him within 50 yards, but this was before heavy shot and ultratight chokes and 3½-inch loads, so

I let him walk.

When he was out of sight I started downhill, too, angling slightly away from his line of travel and moving fast, hoping to get to the road before he did. I made it, but just barely, and the Roadrunner got to the road before I could close the gap. I had to set up well short of where I wanted to be, and after a half-hour I could tell it wasn't going to work. He had made his mark.

I was trying to figure out what to do when I heard a soft, questioning cluck from behind my right shoulder, and moments later a two-year-old gobbler walked into my line of sight, heading down the road toward the bigger bird.

It was my last day to hunt for the season, so the decision was an easy one. When the walk-on bird went behind a tree trunk I made my move, and the Roadrunner's next gobble was at the roar of my 870.

I've never been back to that zig-zag road, and the passage of time lessens the chance that I ever will. These days, my old knees wouldn't like that mountainside very much. If I could keep a gobbler on my level on that hellish slope I could stand it, but that probably wouldn't happen. The Roadrunner is long gone, no question, but I'm betting he passed on some of his tricks to his descendants.

7

Marconi

Turkeys don't operate on schedules and deadlines. Neither should turkey hunters, if they want to fill many tags. Because of that truism, I know better than to go turkey hunting on a morning when I have an obligation that's going to force me to quit early. But that morning I did it anyway, and it cost me a gobbler.

I'd already hunted this turkey a couple times, and while I hadn't yet assigned him Bad Bird status, he was beginning to get under my skin. His home range centered on a long finger ridge with mature hardwoods on top, a wide strip of old cedars lining the sides, and pasture all the way around the bottom, and while he didn't seem to be particularly cagey or sadistic, I still hadn't quite figured him out. He seemed to spend most of his time in the open hardwoods on top of the ridge, but I'd also heard and seen him in the pastures on either side, and pre-season scouting expeditions, not to mention tracks and droppings, revealed he spent some time in the cedars, too.

The two times I'd hunted him, he'd worked to my calling in the hardwoods. I'd seen him both times, but both times he stayed out of gun range and eventually disappeared. After giving him a few days off, I was back for Round Three.

This particular morning, he was roosted farther up the mountain than normal. I could hear him, but he was a long way off. Ordinarily I'd have closed the distance, but there was a rough hollow between us, and I'd broken one of my cardinal rules: I'd scheduled an appointment on the same morning of a turkey hunt. I absolutely *had* to be back to the house by 8:30. I knew it would take a good chunk of time to get up there with the turkey, and if I went to him I'd also have to quit much earlier. Anyway, I reasoned, I was already in his wheelhouse. Maybe he'd come to me.

So I stood pat and listened to him gobble, itching to go to him but knowing better. After a while, I could tell that sure enough, the gobbler was getting closer. Then he started answering my calls in earnest and closing the gap even more.

Maybe this is going to work out, I thought.

But he didn't come up onto the flat ridgetop where I'd worked him the other two hunts and where I was waiting for him now. Instead, he hung up just off the flat, on my side of the cedar belt. He was far enough down the slope so I couldn't see him, but too close for me to risk making a move. The pressing thing was, he didn't arrive below the edge until 7:15, and that gave me no more than 45 minutes to get him killed and tagged and over my shoulder.

I'd been a turkey hunter much too long to think you can rush a turkey, but given the looming deadline I tried to rush him anyway. The results were predictable: I hung him up.

It was a stalemate, with him gobbling and me calling, and I kept looking at my watch and desperately sending him telepathic commands to show himself. He was easily killable, if only I could see him. I looked at my watch. It was 7:35. An hour later, it was 7:42. Another hour went by. 7:47.

I'd been really pouring it on him, and he liked it but wasn't coming any closer. So I did what my late friend Parker Whedon used to advise. I "laid a heavy dose of silence on him."

He increased his already considerable gobbling, and at 7:51 he started moving east below the break of the slope, getting farther away. When he finally climbed the slope, stood on a rock and let me see him, he was 58 yards away. This I know because I later measured it.

It was now 7:56. The gobbler stood like a statue on that

Marconi spent most of his time in the woods, but I'd also seen and heard him in the pastures.

damned rock while I looked down the gun barrel at him and those last four minutes drained away. I tried to convince myself I could kill him, but I knew it was too far. So I watched him helplessly, and then did something I had never done before, and hope never to do again: I stood up, with the gobbler in full sight, and walked off the ridge toward my truck.

Ironically, it was a turkey-related obligation that pulled me away from that gobbler. My first turkey book, *Turkey Hunting Digest*, had just been released, and I was scheduled to be on a live outdoor radio show to talk about it. This was before widespread cell phone usage, and I had to be at the house to use the land line. I barely made it before the phone rang, and after stumbling half-coherently through the radio show and saying goodbye, I raced back to the ridge and tried to get something going with the gobbler.

It was bumping up against 10:00 when I got him to answer me, but he was down in the north pasture and still spooky from our earlier encounter. Or something. At any rate, I couldn't do anything with him. I left him at 1 p.m., still gobbling occasionally from the pasture. That's when I named him Marconi, after the inventor of radio. Because I had to be on a radio show, get it? Okay, it's lame, but there it is anyway.

I rested him for two days, then went back for one last try. There were only a few days left in the season, and I had to leave that afternoon for an out-of-state hunt.

Again he was gobbling from farther up the mountain, close to where he'd been the day I had to leave him. But this time I had no obligations or deadlines, so I crossed the hollow and got over there with him.

I shouldn't have done it. I set up in a place he didn't want to be, and I couldn't change his mind. He went by me by with considerable conversation but no bending of his path. He crossed the hollow, marched right out into the mature oaks on top of the finger ridge and stopped within 50 yards of where I'd had to walk away from him on Radio Day. All I could do was sit there and shake my head. It was a place I knew he favored, and like a fool, I'd left it.

With the gobbler already out there in the open woods of the flat ridgetop, there was no way I could sneak onto the flat with him. So I set up under the break of the hill, and although he gobbled at me for most of the morning, he wouldn't take a peek over the edge so I could shoot him.

When everything got quiet about 11:30, I did some peeking myself. The open woods were as empty as my head, and I went home to load the truck for my road trip.

8

The Outlaw

It was March 17, 1874 when John and James Younger, of the infamous Younger Gang, got into a deadly shoot-out with Pinkerton detectives near the small river town of Roscoe, Missouri. John Younger and two of the Pinkertons bought the farm that day. More than 130 years later and less than a mile from the monument that marks the scene of that confrontation, I got caught up in a battle with a less famous but equally ornery outlaw. This one, though, wore feathers.

The first morning, he slipped in quiet while I was working another gobbler. The first inkling I had of his presence was when he drummed loudly, directly behind me. He was close, *close*, and all I could do was hold still and hope he'd move into my field of view. But after a few minutes a real hen started yelping, also behind me, and he drifted away. I tried to get shapes on him after he left, but all I did was mess up my chances with the other bird.

The second morning he was gobbling, and so was the one I'd worked the day before. They weren't far apart, so I set up between them on the edge of a pasture, hoping one of them would get jealous and try to steal the hen before the other got there. It almost worked. I had both birds coming, but there was a hog-wire fence in the way, and they decided they'd rather make war than make love. They came together in the pasture but well out of gun range, and I had a front-row seat for a violent, three-minute turkey fight. Wing-whacking, aerial spurring duels, snood-pulling, neck-wrapping, the whole catastrophe. They

Bad Birds 2

They came together in the pasture well out of gun range, and decided they'd rather make war than make love.

were pretty well matched, but finally one bird broke off the fight and made an undignified, running, flapping retreat. The winning gobbler chased him a dozen yards, then watched his foe run out of the pasture. He gobbled to hurry the loser on his way, and presently he started strutting.

I believed then and still believe today the winner was the bird that had come in behind me the day before. I may be wrong, but it's my story and I can tell it the way I want to. Either way, I figured I had him where I wanted him.

You're dead meat now, I remember whispering to myself. I let him strut for a minute or two, then hit him with a couple soft clucks. His reaction wasn't what I expected. He upped periscope, gave the pasture border where I was hiding the stink-eye, and then started walking and pecking. He wasn't in a hurry, but every step took him farther from me and my turkey tag. It took him 25 minutes to cross the pasture and enter the woods on the other side. I never saw or heard him again that day.

Day Three was equally disappointing. More so, actually, considering that I never heard a peep out of the gobbler that had lost the fight. Today, The Outlaw was the only game in town. The only one close enough to get to before fly-down time, at any rate. And I may as well not have bothered.

He gobbled readily enough at my dawn tree call, and I dummied up and waited for him to come to the ground. But he sat in the tree well past reasonable time, and I was just about to ignore my better judgement and call to him again when I heard a hen yelping out there to the left, heading steadily in his direction. The Outlaw heard her, too, and started really leaning into his gobbling. She started yelping louder and walked straight to his roost tree. I heard him fly down, and then nothing else out of him for three hours.

That's when he came in behind me again, drumming. It panned out like it had two days earlier, except this time there wasn't a hen involved. He just faded away on his own, and once I was sure he was gone and could safely move, I wasn't able to locate him again.

All three days I'd been fooling with this turkey, I'd been hearing a talkative gobbler on public land across the river, but I hadn't gone over there because I knew getting to him would involve a two-mile walk through some of the brushiest country in west-central Missouri. But three days of being kicked around by The Outlaw made the brush-busting option seem less objectionable, so the next day I opted for it. The gobbler over there turned out to be a fat, pencil-bearded two-year-old with more testosterone than good sense.

But all the while I was calling this turkey in and killing him, all the while I was tagging him, pacing off the distance, picking up my shotgun hull and smelling it – doing all those post-kill ritualistic things that help fix the event in memory – the Outlaw was gobbling across the river. He gobbled more that morning than the total of the three days I'd hunted him.

The next day was the start of Missouri's second week, and my second turkey tag was in play. I was determined to hang it on the Outlaw.

Two hours after daylight, on the fourth day into my continuing education course with this unpredictable gobbler, I finally thought things were rolling my way. As was his custom, he'd been very vocal on the roost. But today no hen came along to complicate things, and when he flew down he began to act like a killable turkey.

Not an easy one, though. I'd moved on him four or five times as he approached, retreated and flanked me, and though he stayed engaged, on each set-up he'd refused to commit. I'd seen him twice, but each time for only a second or two, and each time at more than 60 yards.

Now, though, I had him inside shotgun range. The only thing that separated the Outlaw's wrinkled noggin from the business end of my 870 was the huckleberry-clad crest of a low ridge. He was just off the crest, gobbling every two minutes and drumming nonstop. In an uncharacteristic show of cooperation, he'd stayed put while I made my last-ditch approach, and I'd been able to use the ridge to help me get tight on him. Having been refused at the other four or five set-ups, I pushed the envelope this time. I'd figured out from past encounters that if I was going to kill him, I'd have to get close.

And I did. Creeping along as slow as a box turtle, I got withing what I judged to be no more than 30 yards.

When I was as close as I thought I could get away with, I stood tall beside a good-sized post oak, got the gun to my shoulder, and waited for him to gobble again. When he did, I put the gun on the sound of that last gobble, clucked softly, and quietly slid the safety when I saw the top of his tail fan appear over the ridgetop.

I put the bead on that tail fan and made one final cluck, this one sharper. Up came his head.

And down went the Outlaw, dead as John Younger.

The original monument, erected on the site of the battle.

The modern Gun Battle at Roscoe monument, erected on the state highway near the site.

9

Minnetonka

Minnetonka was one of those birds that seem impossible to kill. Impossible by fair-chase rules, anyway; every turkey is killable if you're willing to cheat. He was an open-land gobbler, living in the drainage basin of a river in northeastern Wyoming, in an area where a dedicated group of local road-shooters kept everything from antelope to jackrabbits jumpy. When a vehicle stopped on a road anywhere under three-quarters of a mile away, Minnetonka didn't ignore it like a normal turkey would do. Instead, he immediately hightailed it back into the river breaks.

For another thing, he seemed immune to all styles of calling. He wouldn't run from it – at least, not as a rule – but he wouldn't come to it, either. He'd gobble, him being a Merriam's and all, but it was mostly just courtesy stuff and he never put much oomph into it. *Yeah, I'm out here,* he seemed to be saying. *But you gotta come to me if you want to play.*

Roads are generally scarce in that part of the world, but where Minnetonka lived there were three. Two of them paralleled each other, climbing out of the river breaks and onto the prairie about two miles apart, and the third road wound and curved through the sage and short-grass prairie a mile or so from the edge of the breaks, connecting the two parallel roads.

The three roads and the edge of the river breaks defined an area of about 1400 acres, and that land plus whatever portion of the river break country he also utilized made up Minnetonka's spring

Bad Birds 2

Minnetonka was the worst kind of Bad Bird – the kind that spends all his time in the open.

range. It was mostly flat out there and the vegetation was sparse, so he usually wasn't hard to find if you drove the perimeter roads. But you had to keep the truck moving, unless all you wanted to do was look at a running turkey.

The way I hunted him was to drive back and forth until I spotted him, and then keep on driving until I was sure he could no longer see or hear my truck. Then I'd park, use the vegetation and the slight pitch and roll of the terrain to get as close as possible, and try to call him in. He always had hens in the morning, but during the five days I hunted him he was alone in the afternoon and evening.

It made no difference either way. He gobbled more at my calling when he was alone, but he wasn't any more inclined to come. Other gobblers were scarce in that part of the drainage that year, though, and I could always find Minnetonka and could always drag some gobbles out of him. And since hope springs eternal in the heart of the turkey hunter (no matter how little it's justified,) I stayed after him with the irrational persistence of a rat terrier digging under a rotten stump.

But the damned turkey simply would not come.

On my sixth and final morning to hunt Wyoming, I almost scratched him off. My hunting buddy had killed a gobbler in a hard-to-reach section of the breaks the previous day, and he'd heard three or four other gobblers in the area. He offered to take me to the place, and I agreed but decided to make one last early-morning try for Minnetonka before we hiked into the rough breaks after the other birds.

We were driving the perimeter roads just after fly-down time when I spied the stubborn old bird where he'd never been before: just over a little sagebrushy rise in the prairie that hid him from a 200-yard section of the connecting road, about 500 yards out from the connecting road itself. He had six hens.

I couldn't have hunted him in this spot before, because he'd have spooked when the truck failed to re-appear from behind the rise. But with an accomplice to drive the truck, I thought I might have a chance. We kept on driving until we were more than a mile away and out of Minnetonka's sight, then stopped so I could get all my stuff together. Then we drove back, and Minnetonka was still there. When the rise in the landscape took us out of the gobbler's sight my buddy slowed the truck to a crawl and I bailed out onto the dusty road. He kept on going so Minnetonka could see him leave.

I crossed the fence and started up the gentle slope, taking as much advantage of the sparse sage as possible. But the slope was gentle, and it wasn't long before I started seeing sagebrush on the other side of the slope. I knew I was getting pretty close to running out of cover. That's when I spied the top of his tail fan over the top of the rise.

I am a rotund man, no longer built for crawling. But when in the course of human/turkey interactions it becomes prudent for me to crawl, I do it. I was still a hundred yards shy of the crest, and it took a good five minutes to cover it flat on my belly. When I reached the last clump of sage on my side of the crest, though, I heard the unmistakable, nearly subsonic drone of a drumming turkey.

When these battered old eardrums can hear a turkey drumming, that turkey is close. Within shotgun range, usually. So I paused for a moment, caught my breath, steadied my nerves, and rose slowly to my knees behind my little sagebush, gun to my shoulder and safety off.

The first thing I saw was the backside of his extended, perfectly round tail fan, 20 yards away. The second thing I saw was the hen turkey that popped her head over the edge of the rise less than 10 feet from me. She immediately went airborne, and two or three of her sisters quickly followed her. The gobbler ran his head up over his tail fan, alert for danger and preparing to run, but he never got the chance.

I was walking out to take a look at him when I stepped on a sharp rock and it hurt. I looked down, and that's when I realized that in my hurry to get out of the truck, I'd neglected to take off my moccasins and put on my hunting boots.

And that's why I named him Minnetonka.

Minnetonka

10

Sir Edmund

As mountains go, Boulder Mountain isn't big – five square miles tops, depending on what ridges and spurs you decide are part of the mountain. But when you're in an easy chair looking at a topo map, five square miles looks much less impressive than that same amount of real estate looks when you're on your actual feet, on the actual ground, on the actual mountain.

In the case of Boulder, one of the biggest differences is the steepness of its slopes. When those brown contour lines come closer together on a topo map it just makes that part of the page browner. Out there on the landscape, it can give you a heart attack.

There are flat places on Boulder Mountain, sure, as there are on most of the mountains in these parts. But there aren't many, and they aren't big, and they're separated by some of the awfullest stuff you'll find this side of the River Styx: boulder fields, slopes steep as a cow's face and paved with cantaloupe-sized rocks, sheer bluffs, cedar thickets protected much too long from the cleansing effects of fire.

There are also some gentle slopes cloaked with open, pretty stands of big hardwoods, but these are also smallish and relatively scarce. What it amounts to is the mountain consists of maybe 200 acres of easy-to-negotiate habitat nuggeted sparsely into 3,000 acres of Hell.

But that's only part of what I was up against. Another thing was a gobbler that knew every one of those little patches of easy stuff on his side of the mountain and visited them regularly, with no discernible pattern, and didn't like to stay in any of them very long.

He ranged over most of the west half of Boulder Mountain. To the best of my knowledge, he never roosted twice in the same place. Because I had to look for him in several square miles of broken terrain every morning, there were days when I never made contact. But he was an early-gobbling turkey, and he was vocal enough that if I guessed right and was close enough to hear him when he cranked up, I could usually get close enough to set up on him before flydown. Even when I couldn't, he kept gobbling well into the morning, so I could often intercept him and work him.

Sir Edmund ranged over several square miles of Boulder Mountain. This made him hard to find.

I hunted him off and on for three seasons, and made contact 15 times in all. I know it was the same bird because he had a distinctive stutter late in his gobble, almost like a hiccup. Twice during those three seasons I killed walk-on gobblers that came in silently while I was calling to the hiccuping gobbler, but the only time I laid eyes on him in those three seasons was the morning I killed him. But I'm getting ahead of myself.

I've already told you he didn't like to stay in one spot too long, which made getting close to him problematic due to the rough terrain. I usually found myself in the low-percentage position of tagging along behind, calling from places he'd already vacated. The second day I worked him that first season, he flew down onto a small bench, and by the time I got there he'd relocated uphill, to a second bench separated from the first by a 150-foot cliff. The only way he could have gotten up there was fly or climb up through a broken, rocky defile I tried to climb and couldn't. Since I'm pretty sure he didn't fly, I named him after the Englishman who first climbed Everest.

Over the next two seasons Sir Edmund re-earned his name on numerous occasions. More often than not, there were days when I simply could not find a way to follow him around the mountain.

He was an entertaining turkey, though, even if he was a frustrating one. Not once did I come off the mountain thinking I'd had a bad hunt, except maybe on the two or three days when I failed to find him. He'd respond well enough to my calling, and would even come partway to me most of the time. But his itchy-footedness, combined with the mountain's rough terrain, kept me from getting tight enough on him to get inside his comfort zone.

Until that final day. This time, when Sir Edmund started gobbling in the pre-dawn darkness, as was his habit, he was on the same narrow bench with me and less than 300 yards away, much closer than he'd ever been before when he cranked up. Luck of all luck, there was a 10-acre hardwood flat on the bench between us. He was on the north end of the flat, I was on the south, and I'll tell you the truth: I was tempted to sneak through the darkness and roll him off his limb. I'd hunted him fair and square for three seasons, though, and figured it would be a shame to ruin it at the end. I'm not normally that noble, but there it lays. Make of it what you will.

So I eased into my end of the flat, closed the gap and set up within range of a little open spot he'd favored on other hunts, and waited for daylight. He was 125 yards down the bench, and by the time the first tinge of color touched the sky, he'd gobbled a hundred times. I was determined to wait silently, but in the end I couldn't help myself. I gave him a little run of tree yelps...

...and shut him up as effectively as if I'd yelled "Hey, turkey!" and started beating two dish pans together.

He was silent for 25 minutes, and then I heard him fly down. Ten minutes later he still hadn't said anything, and I came to the rueful conclusion I'd blown it with Sir Edmund for that day.

But then I remembered: on the two previous occasions I'd worked him on this flat, he'd left it in favor of a similar flat on the next bench up the mountain, and for once the second destination was pretty easy to reach. So I backed out, climbed to the next bench and eased quietly into the south end of the new hardwood flat. I was just sitting down when Sir Edmund hiccuped his familiar gobble less than 75 yards away, just out of sight under the lip of the bench.

I barely had time to shoulder my gun when his blue and white head came into sight at 60 yards. He stopped with just his head showing and carefully looked things over. After what seemed like an hour but could only have been a minute or two, his head disappeared. A few seconds later Sir Edmund was up there with me, strutting through a patch of sunlight at 45 yards. He was angling toward me on a path that would have brought him within 25 yards, but I didn't wait that long and shot him at 30.

If I've ever killed a gobbler worthy of the title "Sir", it was this one. Boulder Mountain still has turkeys; matter of fact, I killed one there last spring. But there'll never be another Sir Edmund.

At least, I hope not.

Bad Birds 2

11

Harry S

When a turkey's head is only four feet downrange, it's not an easy target to hit with a tightly-choked shotgun. That's why it didn't surprise me when I missed this one. After the gobbler flew the river, after my adrenaline rush subsided, after things got quiet again, the playback in my head reminded me of those pop-up targets at a county fair shooting gallery. Except that I only got the one shot.

But I'm getting ahead of you. From the top:

The sprawling central Missouri reservoir known as Truman Lake was named for President Harry S Truman, famous for his "if you can't stand the heat, get out of the kitchen" remark and his "The Buck Stops Here" desk plaque. I go there most years (to the lake, not the Oval Office) to chase turkeys on the abundant public land.

Usually there are enough birds to make things interesting, but not this year. In three days I hadn't worked a gobbler. Hadn't even heard many, and most of those were either across the lake, were being worked by other hunters, or were the kind that give you a couple gobbles to get you moving toward them, then shut up before you arrive.

All three mornings, though, I'd been hearing one bird gobbling from a steep bluff across the lake. He was on Corps of Engineers land, but the public strip wasn't very wide and was almost completely landlocked by private land. I could have reached him easily if I'd been an otter, or if I'd had permission to cross the private, but neither was the case. The only ways to reach him were by boat, which I didn't have, or by skirting the lakeshore from an access point nearly three miles down the lake. I'd made the trek once before, and it was no picnic: rocky, steep slopes, dense brush, and a long, unpleasant hike.

But when you're in a turkey drought, three days of steady gobbling from the same place exerts a powerful pull. That's why, well before daylight on the fourth morning, I found myself clawing through that three miles of dense brush in the dark, headed toward the stomping ground of the noisy gobbler I'd already named for our 33rd president.

Negotiating dense cover in the dark makes for slow going, and I hadn't allowed myself quite enough time. He was already on the ground before I got close enough to hear him, and he was really tearing it up. Sure enough, he was on the private land, but he was still close enough to the public boundary to set up on him. I soon had him coming my way.

The private land in question was mostly flat pasture, interspersed with small woodlots and thickets. By contrast, the adjoining government land dropped off steep, beginning almost at the boundary, and fell more than 100 feet to the lake. I figured the gobbler would walk the property line, but there was a 20-yard strip of level ground on the public before the hill broke. I hoped he'd be on my side of the line when he came in.

He didn't stay up on the flat, though, as I expected. Instead, he dropped about halfway down the timbered slope, set up his bandstand, and held a one-turkey concert for the next two hours. I moved on him four times, trying to break him loose, but he stood pat. It was past nine o'clock when I heard the hens coming, one from each direction. He shut up and didn't gobble again before quitting time at 1 p.m.

The next morning I started earlier, and this time I was within 300 yards when he made his first gobble. He was roosted in a big red oak in the middle of the private pasture. It was an unapproachable lie, since there was nothing but grass in all directions, and private land besides. I got as close as I could, about 200 yards, and set up so I could see the flat pasture and also over the edge of the hill and down toward

Harry S

Harry probably wouldn't have been a Bad Bird at all, if he hadn't stayed on the wrong side of the line so much.

the lake.

This morning, though, he stayed in the tree well after daylight. By the time he flew down there were several hens under him. They took him away across the pasture. Even with the three-mile hike back to the truck, I still had time to go elsewhere, and I got lucky and killed a suicidal two-year-old about eleven o'clock that morning.

The pressure was now off, but still I could feel the heat from Harry's kitchen. So I went back to him on the final morning of my Missouri hunt. I had to be in Nebraska that evening, but figured I could give Harry another two or three hours before starting the long drive.

It didn't take that long.

He wasn't in the big tree in the pasture, but rather on the downslope near the lake. I was able to set up right above him, no more than 75 yards away. At daylight, I could see him gobbling and strutting on his limb, almost level with my position on top of the ridge. I gave him a tree yelp to get him thinking my way, and when he cut me off, I smiled and shifted the diaphragm into my cheek.

He flew down straight at me, but landed below the steep break of the hill and out of sight. I could hear him drumming and dragging his wings, though, and knew he was very, very close.

I was tracking the sound with my gun barrel, nervous as a Chihuahua, when things went silent. I hate that, especially when a bird is that close. As usual, I got antsy and screwed it up. After what seemed like 30 minutes but was probably only 5 or 10, I decided I needed to make another call. I worked up some moisture and made a soft, questioning *cluck?* That's when hell got unleashed.

The turkey gobbled in my face, a thunderous, deep-throated roar with a lot of bottom in it. The sound was 30 degrees left of my gun barrel. I moved the gun immediately, but too late; he was so close to the top all he had to do was raise his head and see me, and he caught me making the move. I shot as he ducked, and the marble-sized swarm of shot that was my pattern whizzed past his head. He flew, I cussed, I kicked at the ground, I threw my hat down and stomped on it.

The heat was too much to stand; it was time to get out of the kitchen. I was in Nebraska well before dark.

12

Lazybones

When you park at the side of the Forest Service-slash-county road where the old WPA bridge spans the creek, you have choices. You can go upstream or downstream. You can go in on the east or west side of the creek. You can go up on the ridges, or you can stay in the creek bottom. It's all good turkey country. You also have the option of staying at the bridge and listening for gobbling before deciding which direction to go, but that's what most everybody else does. As a consequence, the birds close to the bridge get fooled with a lot.

It's a big creek bottom, though, both wide and long, and there's plenty of room to walk past the realm of the road hunters and get into less-pressured real estate. I'd hunted all four quadrants before, but it had been a while – four or five years, maybe more. With no advance scouting intelligence available, it was a guessing game. So I eenie-meenie-miney-mo'ed it. Upstream, west side of the creek, in the creek bottom.

A mile in, I stopped to rest and wait for daylight. As so often happens, the only gobbler I heard was on the east side of the creek and a long way off. But he seemed to be the only game in town, so I did what turkey hunters do: I waded the waist-deep creek and went to him.

As it turned out, I needn't have waded. He stayed on the roost so long I would've had time to walk back to the bridge and return along the east side of the creek. But I didn't know that at the time, so I waded, got as close as I dared in the growing dawn light and made my set.

Three hours later I was still sitting there, clammy and cold, and the turkey was still in his roost tree, gobbling twice a minute. Finally, another hunter came in on him from the opposite side, got too close, and flushed him. It's maybe the only time in my life I've been glad to have interference from another hunter.

I figured the turkey would start gobbling again after a while, so I moseyed in the direction he'd flown. I sat around in the creek bottom until noon, moving here and there, calling soft and loud, and as far as I know he never made another peep.

That was on a Sunday. Monday morning found me back in the creek bottom, but now I was east of the creek. He started gobbling in the dark, pretty close to where he'd been the day before, and again I was able to get in pretty close. A little too close, really. When daylight came, I could see him 70 yards away on a big horizontal limb of a massive swamp chestnut oak, gobbling, strutting and walking back and forth on the limb.

Once again he seemed in no hurry to come to the ground, and once again I sat there for hours and watched him fool around in the tree. This time, though, there was no other hunter to rescue me, so I had to wait him out. He finally pitched down at 9 a.m., angling toward me but lighting out of range and out of sight behind a plum thicket. He answered my run of yelps, but I could tell his heart wasn't in it. He gobbled three times on the ground over the next half-hour, each time farther away. I chased him, but it was useless.

I went to him Tuesday morning and again sat pinned down until midmorning. It was becoming obvious that it was a waste of time to try hunting this gobbler off the roost. So I went elsewhere Wednesday morning, got beat by a more conventional gobbler in a more conventional way, and eased into the creek bottom about two o'clock that afternoon.

All three days I'd hunted Lazybones, he'd gone upstream

when he finally left the tree. So I went a quarter-mile past his favored roosting area before stopping to look for a likely set-up spot. I found a good one: two old log roads came together in a V just north of a small tributary of the main creek, and I could sit at the base of a big shortleaf pine on a slight rise on the south side of the creek and cover both converging roads at a range of 35 yards, with good elevation to improve my set.

I heard him gobble at 3:30, way north of me, about as far away as it's possible for me to hear a turkey. My first impulse was to close the gap, but I resisted and stood pat. My set-up was as good as I could hope for, and I had time to wait.

It was a good decision. The next time he gobbled, at 3:50, he was only 300 yards away, but farther west toward the main creek. He didn't answer my return yelp, but he gobbled again at 4:10 and now he was 200 yards out and to my right. If he continued his present course he'd get by me to the east. I got up, quickly crossed the tributary to the V of the logging roads, and staged a short turkey fight with two push-button calls and a mouth diaphragm. He gobbled twice during the turkey fight, and I barely made it back to my set-up tree before he gobbled again, this time inside 100 yards and sounding like he meant it.

I got the gun on my knee and waited, confident and patient as a Marine sniper. Twenty minutes later, both confidence and patience were beginning to waver. That's when the coarse, questioning *cluck?* came from hard off my right shoulder. It was close. Much too close.

I somehow managed to keep from flinching, and when I cranked my eyeballs around as far as they would go, I could see a black, out-of-focus blur standing erect and motionless at 15 yards. There was nothing to do but keep still; at that range, any movement on my part would have put him into panic mode. Lazybones clucked at me one more time, and again I managed to not flinch. I was pretty proud of myself, despite the hairiness of the situation, but I knew I was a long way from winning the encounter.

But my adversary helped me out. Not panicked but suspicious, he decided he needed to leave, but his mistake was he decided to do so via the logging road that crossed the tributary in front of me. His sixth or seventh step brought him in front of my gun barrel at 10 yards, and I waited until he doubled the distance between us before sending a dense swarm of 5s through the buggy, shadowy afternoon woods. His warty head intercepted a good portion of that shot swarm, and Lazybones hit the ground for the last time.

Lazybones had a good reason for sleeping late. He was a senior citizen turkey.

13

The Bluff Dweller

Not far north of Antlers, a curving backbone of granite cuts an arc through the arid, scrubby stuff that passes for forest in southeast Oklahoma. It looks like anything but good turkey country, but for a few years in the 1980s I found some pretty decent hunting there.

It was paper company land but this was before leasing became the norm, so it got hunted pretty hard. Therefore, the ridge had its share of bad birds. One rainy April morning I met one of them. I'd been on a pair of hard-gobbling turkeys early that morning, before the rain started, but when things turned nasty they dummied up. Nowadays, when it starts to rain like that, I quit and head for the truck. But this was in my hard-charging, to-hell-with-the-weather years, so I kept right on hunting. I spent the next three or four hours slipping and sliding around the ridge in a more or less steady downpour, trying unsuccessfully to get something going.

Finally, wet as a muskrat and cold as a frog, I found shelter in the lee of a 15-foot rock bluff that separated two benches on the east side of the ridge. By sitting cross-legged and hunching my shoulders forward, I could fit into a square-yard dry spot under a low overhanging ledge. After eating my lunch (a ham, cheese and rainwater sandwich,) I sat there a while like a marooned sailor, then tried to nap. I was too uncomfortable for that. Bored and cold, I dug out a split-reed diaphragm and started calling as loud as I could, running clucks, yelps, cutts and cackles together in the awfullest racket you ever heard.

Somewhere in the middle of it, I thought I heard a turkey

gobble. I shut up and listened: nothing but rain.

After a while I started calling again, and this time I was sure I heard it: a turkey was answering me. I got a line on him this time, but it was bad news. The gobbler was directly behind and above me, on the bench above the rock bluff under which I was hiding. With the rain and the bluff interfering with my hearing, I wasn't sure how far away he was, and I needed that bit of intelligence before deciding if I could move away from the vertical wall and maybe get up on the bench with him.

So I called again, and the turkey nearly blew my hat off. He was directly above me now, near the edge of the bluff, probably no more than 20 feet away. But he might as well have been on an asteroid for all the chance I had of killing him, because there was an asteroid's worth of granite ledge between his head and the business end of my shotgun.

The rain, which had been steady but moderate for the past hour, now decided to ramp it up a notch. The purling hiss of gentle rain became the surging roar of a monsoon, and my cramped overhang was suddenly the space behind a waterfall. It was like a tiny version of that place where Daniel Day Lewis got separated from Madeleine Stowe in *The Last of the Mohicans*.

But that simile didn't occur to me at the time because the movie hadn't been made yet. Anyway, I didn't have anything pretty to look at like Madeleine Stowe. So I just saw it as being stuck in a hole, and by the time the rain let up 15 minutes later, my gobbler was gone. Despite my best efforts I couldn't raise him again. I wondered if maybe he'd gotten washed off the face of planet Earth.

The next day the rain had moved on, but it left a clammy, foggy morning in its wake. The old-timers used to say a wet turkey won't gobble, and though I later found the old timers to be full of misinformation, this time they were spot on. I'd heard seven gobblers the previous morning; today nobody made a peep. I spent most of the morning looking without success for a gobbler to play with. At about

The Bluff Dweller

The Bluff Dweller didn't play fair. But what else would you expect from a Bad Bird?

11 a.m., I found myself in the neighborhood of the overhanging ledge and decided to sit there a while and eat another somewhat less soggy ham sandwich. For old time's sake, you know.

This time, though, I sat on top of the bluff, with my legs dangling over the side. It proved unwise. I was halfway through my lunch when a turkey gobbled behind me, fairly close. Too close, in fact, to let me get up and move to a good set-up spot. So I played the hand I was dealt: I rolled over onto my stomach, feet hanging out into space, and pointed my shotgun toward the enemy. The gobbler cut off my first run of yelps, and two seconds later he stepped out from behind a tree. At 75 yards.

And that's where he stayed for the next 30 minutes, standing like a statue and looking for the hen that was supposed to be standing there looking back at him. I was flat on my belly, an uncomfortable and rarely effective set-up position, and I was pinned down like a grasshopper in a sophomore's bug collection. When he started moving it was a flanking maneuver to my left; more bad news, since I shoot southpaw. He was in full sight the whole time and never gave me a chance to swap shoulders with the gun, so I tracked him with my barrel as far as my prone position would let me. It wasn't far enough. By the time he was in gun range he was 30 degrees past my swing radius, and although I could still see him out of my left eye, he still might as well have been on that damn asteroid.

After a long while he walked off along the edge of the bluff, not spooked, in no hurry, just leaving. When he was out of sight I dropped to the lower bench, made a big loop and got on him again, but I couldn't do anything more with him. He followed the bluff all the way out of hearing, gobbling occasionally but not at me, and that was it for the day.

I failed to make contact with him the third morning, but the day after that, he was gobbling in the vicinity of the rock ledge at 8 a.m. I set up within 50 yards of the uphill side of the bluff and worked him for 90 minutes, during which time I saw him twice at 75 yards.

But he wouldn't commit, and the encounter ended as the others had, with him getting tired of the whole mess and going away along the contour of the bluff. On the way back to camp I ran into a suicidal two-year-old I think I could have killed with a baseball bat. The two-minute flash hunt lifted my drooping spirits, and the next morning I was back near the rock ledge. It was the final day of my Oklahoma hunt, and renewed of vigor, I was determined to (a) kill this turkey or (b) go down swinging.

At first, things looked promising. He was roosted not far from the bluff, and this was the first day I'd gotten on him early. The first part of the encounter was unremarkable: he gobbled enough on the limb, not too much, not too little, and flew down about when he should have, and approached my calling with the proper amount of enthusiasm and speed.

But he stopped out there at that 75-yard mark that seemed to be the boundary of his personal comfort zone. I could see him, but I couldn't do anything about it. Two hours later he faded away and went out of sight. As soon as I could safely move, I backed off, dropped under the bluff and hustled 200 yards to the other side of him before climbing back up onto the higher bench and making another set.

I never heard or saw him again, so in the end it was it was (b).

Lucky was always surrounded by a retinue of hens and jakes

14

Lucky

The first time I saw him was Opening Day, and I could have killed him then but for one thing. Well, actually five things, and he was surrounded by them: a retinue of three hens and two jakes. All six turkeys were in a big wad, and I couldn't shoot the big boy without running the risk of killing another turkey or two.

He came to me that first day along an abandoned fence line, walking a plowed firebreak at the edge of a brushy old-field site, while I waited in the edge of the bigger woods a dozen yards outside the fence. I couldn't see him coming because of the brush along my side, and until he came into sight at 30 yards, I thought he was alone. He came by me at less than 20 yards, but his entourage of lesser birds never gave me the clear shot I needed. Despite the two or three soft, then louder, then still louder clucks I made to make him stop, he never did. Most of the little flock was well past me when a sharp-eyed old hen picked me out and started making alarm noises. They didn't exactly bolt, but they picked up their pace, and all I could do was watch helplessly as they disappeared into the brush. *You're a lucky bird,* I thought, and presto, there was his name.

I had several other places I wanted to check, so for the next three days I hunted elsewhere. But when I came back to the brushy old-field edge on the season's fifth day, Lucky was strutting along the firebreak next to the fence, apparently with the same hens and jakes. At least, the numbers were the same. He wasn't gobbling and I didn't know they were there, but sometimes I'm lucky, too, and I spotted them first. They were about 200 yards away, and I was able to halve the distance by moving up through the thick woods on my side of the firebreak.

I took my time choosing a set-up that would let me see farther along the fence than my set-up on the first encounter. When I called, Lucky double-gobbled, and a few minutes later the whole bunch was in sight at 80 yards. The big bird intensified his strut, waiting for me to show myself. When I didn't, he started a back-and-forth pattern of movement, moving five or six yards my way, then drifting back to his pod of hens. He was interested, but he'd evidently heard what they say about the value of a bird in the hand. And he had three.

The arithmetic wasn't in my favor, but over the next 45 minutes I made some progress anyway. Every time he went back to his hens, I gave him some more sweet talk. Each time he came back toward me, and he got a little closer every time. It was becoming apparent he *really* wanted me to come join his little party. It would have been comical if the stakes hadn't been so high.

Finally I got one of the hens interested in talking to me, and she started moseying my way. The other turkeys followed, with Lucky riding drag. She wasn't aggressive, just chatty, and we were getting along fairly well, swapping recipes or something, I don't know.

She was within 35 yards and I was waiting for the longbeard to catch up with her. He was still on the wrong side of the 50-yard mark when an armadillo came into the firebreak, rooting along inside the bubble of oblivion that seems to surround these critters. The turkeys didn't exactly spook, but they did alter their course, and when they came by me this time they were 45 yards from the fence and well into the brush. Once again I couldn't get the gobbler to stop and raise his head during the two or three times he was in the clear. It's unwise to shoot a strutting gobbler at that range, especially in brush, so once again I let him walk. It was beginning to get old.

A friend was coming in that afternoon to hunt for a few days, and over glasses of brown liquid that night we decided a double-team hunt was in order. Next morning, sure as sunrise, Lucky was out there strutting on the firebreak with his hens and jakes. Robert set up as close as possible to the group of turkeys, and I backed off down the fenceline and started calling. Lucky was answering and getting closer, and although I couldn't see him, I was thinking he ought to be getting close to Robert's position.

When the gun went off, turkeys went in every direction. Unfortunately, Lucky was one of them. When I got to where Robert was standing, he was emitting a low, steady rumble of words I'm pretty sure he didn't learn in Sunday school.

"He was too damn close," Robert said when I got him calmed down enough to talk. "I couldn't shoot the (deleted) when he was out there in the kill zone because of all the (deleted) hens, and then when he got in tight I got a chance when he was less than five yards away. He moved his (deleted) head just as I shot, and I missed the (deleted) clean."

We rested the (deleted) the next day and went back to try him again the day after that. This time I was the front man and Robert was the caller, but after getting his ears rung ol' Lucky wasn't having any of it. He'd stand down there and gobble back, but when he started moving it was the other way. We chased him and his hens for nearly a mile along the edge of that old field, but we couldn't turn him around and eventually lost him.

Robert had to leave that afternoon, so I went back to hunt Lucky one more time before leaving for an out-of-state hunt. I hunted him solo like I had in the beginning, but this time I got there early and set out a jake and hen decoy in breeding position. I don't like using decoys, but occasionally I backslide.

Lucky started gobbling in the woods on the other side of the half-mile-wide old field, and since I was a long way from him I really leaned into the calling. He liked it, and before long I could tell he was on the ground and moving my way.

When he popped out into the firebreak, he was about 150 yards from the decoys, and I was 40 yards closer to him than they were. Catbird seat. He gobbled as soon as he saw the jake. Somehow I managed to stay quiet.

He was still with the three hens, but the jakes were absent. I don't know if that was the key or it was the decoys, but this time he didn't hesitate. Here he came, neck as red as a cardinal, head as white as a softball.

I had my gun on him at 60 yards and was already congratulating myself on my turkey hunting acumen when he slicked down and darted into the brush. Seconds later, two fat guys in camouflage came riding down the firebreak on a red side-by-side four-wheeler. This on public land, where motorized vehicles were prohibited off-road.

They never saw Lucky because he was already gone, but they did finally spy my two decoys when they were less than 40 yards from them. They were precisely even with my set-up in the edge of the woods, and one of them picked me out at a range of five yards. They stopped, grinned (as if there was something funny about the situation,) waved, turned around and left.

When my race on earth is run and I'm wrangling with St. Peter at the Pearly Gates, I'm going to use as a bargaining chip the fact that I didn't shoot their tires out.

It ought to count for something.

15

Woodrow Too

On a winter afternoon in 1962, Woodrow Dixon watched approvingly as a dozen wild turkeys flew across Button River from his 200-acre south pasture in rural Copiah County, Mississippi. The birds had been trapped that morning by wildlife biologists in the Mississippi River bottoms four hours northwest, and they were the first turkeys ever released in Copiah and the surrounding counties.

Woodrow Dixon died in March, 2011, before Jill and I had a chance to meet him. But he'd been friend and mentor to our friend and fellow outdoor writer Bobby Dale, and we'd been hearing Woodrow stories for years. Bobby had arranged an invitation from Woodrow's grandson Clark for us to hunt this hallowed ground. Fifty years after that historic turkey release, I stood at that exact spot in the south pasture and listened to a descendant of those birds gobbling his head off.

The pasture, once home to Woodrow's cattle, was now a pasture in name only. Now it was a nearly mature pine plantation, and it had been carefully thinned the previous December. The thinning had opened the stand considerably, and the gobbler was out there in the middle of it. I got as close as I could, but I was running a little late and he was already on the ground and gobbling when I got out of the truck. The open woods and growing daylight kept me from getting as tight as I wanted.

Naturally, a hen got to him before I could get him coming my way. He kept gobbling at me but refused to leave her, and the open nature of the thinned pines made it impossible to get inside his comfort zone. The hen and I got into a pretty good catfight, but it was all long-distance. The turkeys and I maneuvered around the plantation for an hour or two and then they just wandered off. He gobbled intermittently until about 10 o'clock, just enough to keep me from going elsewhere. The last time I heard him, he'd crossed Button River about where the 1962 turkeys had crossed, then headed upstream though the cool, shady bottom.

The next morning I hunted elsewhere at first light and heard several turkeys, but all of them were on property I didn't have permission to hunt. So I went back to the south pasture at 8:30, and the turkey gobbled only 200 yards away as I was getting my stuff out of the truck. Again, he was in the plantation pines. But he'd heard the vehicle when I drove in, and while it didn't spook him, he wouldn't come that way. I circled him, but again I couldn't set up close enough because of the open understory.

Same song, different verse. He gobbled, I called. A hen yelped, I called. He gobbled. Nobody came. We waltzed around the pasture some more. The gobbler again crossed Button River, went upstream, and quit gobbling about 10:30.

Nobody ever accused me of being a quick study. The next morning, instead of setting up down by the river where the gobbler was telling me he wanted to go, I got in above him again. For the third time in a row, he kept me hanging for a couple hours, then drifted away, crossed the river, headed upstream, and shut up.

I'd previously named another turkey Woodrow, after Captain Woodrow Call in *Lonesome Dove* (chapter 39 in the first *Bad Birds* book.) But really, what else could I name this one? When the gobbler left me that third time, by definition he became a Bad Bird, and officially he became Woodrow Too.

While Woodrow Too had been whipping my butt, my wife and Bobby Dale were hunting another part of the Dixon property, but they hadn't been hearing much. So we all descended on the 200-acre south pasture that afternoon to see if we couldn't conquer this cantankerous bird through sheer numbers. Bobby hunted along the north line, Jill went to the old release site along the east boundary, and I headed south – upstream – along Button River, in the direction the turkey had gone the last three mornings. Stopping every 50 yards or so and calling softly, I moseyed slowly through the unfamiliar terrain, trying to make contact without bumping anybody.

Bobby had told me the Dixons' south boundary was marked with red paint, and the land beyond was off limits. I could see a splash of red on a beech trunk 75 yards ahead when Woodrow Too gobbled. He wasn't far past the paint but across Button River.

I circled left and crossed the stream (as rivers go, the Button ain't much,) cut the distance a little, and set up on the edge of a cool, shady draw. Woodrow Too was farther up the draw, and he cut my first call with a gobble that was decidedly more animated than the four or five gobbles he'd uttered while I was getting into position.

I had more cover to work with than I'd had in the south pasture, so even though the gobbler was fairly close I immediately moved to a new calling position. When he answered me again, I moved again. Neither move covered more than 25 yards, and neither brought me closer to the turkey; I just didn't want to do all my calling from the same place when I had another option.

After one more move I sat down for good on the highest ground on the west edge of the draw. Woodrow Too started my way when I called, quickly closing the distance from 100 yards to about 50. But that's where he hung up. That's the outer edge of effective range for my 870, but only if the turkey is in the clear. This one wasn't. I could see him the whole time, but never the whole bird. He gobbled some, but mostly he drummed, and the natural amphitheater amplified and enriched the sound. For the next 20 minutes I listened to the clearest, strongest drumming my battered old eardrums had enjoyed in 15 years.

I'd been silent all that time, but I was scared he was about to leave. I didn't want to run a box or slate because of the necessary movement, but I had a raspy diaphragm in my mouth, and I decided to give him a little encouragement.

What I intended to be a short run of soft, contented yelps somehow got away from me. To my horror, what came out of my mouth turned out to be an aggressive, barking yelp-cutt combo, I suppose it was a manifestation of the suspense of the moment and of my frustration from the past three mornings.

Whatever, it was pretty loud stuff. As close as he was, I figured I'd blown it. But instead of leaving, Woodrow Too double-gobbled, gobbled again three seconds later, and then broke the hang-up. He came slow, but he came. I had enough sense to shut up and let him. I picked out an opening at 30 yards, and when he came into it I gave him a sharp cluck. He stopped, and I tipped him over.

For a south Mississippi gobbler, this one was a whopper: 20 pounds, with a thick 10½-inch beard and 1¼-inch spurs. Soon afterward, I laid him down for photos at the site of that long-ago release. Jill was hunting the pasture and grumbled some about her late-afternoon hunt getting messed up, but she later killed plenty of gobblers that season so maybe she'll eventually forgive me that one transgression.

But forgiveness or not, I could no more have passed up the chance to take a picture with him at the site of that first release than I could have resisted naming him Woodrow Too.

Woodrow Too

Woodrow Too was a whopper for a south Mississippi gobbler.

16

She

Pre-season scouting, late March, mid-morning, beautiful weather. I was driving to one of my favorite hunting spots to check for sign when I topped a rise and found the Forest Service road in front of me full of turkeys.

There were two longbeards, at least three jakes and a whole squadron of hens, all mixed together. One bird was white as a snowy egret, with a thin 4-inch beard poking through the white feathers. It seemed to be too small for a gobbler, even a jake gobbler, but all the turkeys were in simultaneous motion trying to get out of my way. I wasn't sure what I was looking at. They didn't stand around while I parsed it out, either.

Several days later I came through there again and saw the same flock of turkeys – this time in a pasture 50 yards off the road. This time they were segregated into the normal subgroups – gobblers strutting, jakes skulking nearby, hens pecking around ignoring the gobblers. The white bird was in with the hens, settling the gender question.

A white, bearded hen. Quite an unusual bird. Only about two percent of wild turkey hens have beards, I'm told, and scarcer still are white birds in the wild. So I was looking at a bird in…what? Ten thousand? A hundred thousand? At the time, bearded hens were legal in my home state, but we also have a six-inch beard minimum and I knew she wouldn't make the cut. Therefore, it didn't enter my head to hunt this bird. Not that spring, anyway.

I saw her three times during the season, twice with the two

longbeards. The second time, I called the two longbeards away from her and killed one of them. The third time I saw her was late in the season, and She was by herself.

During the summer I saw her twice, by herself both times. Evidently, She hadn't produced any chicks, and considering her coloration, I wasn't surprised. I didn't have much faith in the idea of her being able to hide from predators long enough to incubate a clutch of eggs.

The following March, She was back in the same area, with another mixed flock of turkeys near where I'd first seen her. By this time her beard length had doubled, to more than eight inches. I started thinking how nice She'd look mounted in my office, and decided that when the season opened, I'd try to hang one of my tags on her pink leg.

Okay, let's hit the pause button and get something straight here: Don't waste your time, and don't waste mine. Don't write me, all hot and bothered, to berate me for my callow decision to kill a hen. I don't want to hear it. This was a legal turkey, and I'd already had the pro-and-con argument with myself. Her glaring coloration put her at a disadvantage for nesting – indeed, for her very survival. I was surprised she'd lasted into her second year. She was a rare trophy and I wanted her. It was a personal decision, arrived at after considerable internal debate, and I don't need to hear any guff about it.

So. Back to the story:

Judging from the number of times I'd seen her, I figured She'd be pretty easy to kill. I figured wrong.

Opening day, I saw her with a single gobbler and five hens on the back side of a pasture beside the road, 300 yards from where I'd seen her that first time the year before. I stayed with them for three hours, calling from three or four set-ups around the edge of the pasture, but couldn't get her close enough. The gobbler was killable for more than five minutes, and to that point it was the only time in my life I'd ever laid off shooting a tom while waiting for a hen.

I went back that afternoon, and found her in the pasture with two of the hens. The gobbler had gone off somewhere to tend other traplines.

Now She'll be easy, I thought, but again I was wrong. I called the two brown hens within 20 yards, but the white one stayed out there in the middle, and when She left the field at sundown She did it by crossing the road opposite my set-up.

The second day I couldn't find her. Nor the third. I decided to try one more time before going elsewhere to hunt, and on the fourth day I watched her fly down with three brown hens. When I started calling, they all started coming my way. They were almost close enough, and would have been if She'd been on the front edge of the group instead of dragging along behind. But then a longbeard walked into the field 150 yards away and gobbled twice, and the hens lost interest in me and went to him.

I went back to the truck and spent the rest of the morning hunting a gobbler I'd been hearing from my front porch. About noon, he walked silently into my set-up and I killed him.

With the pressure off, I decided to save my second Arkansas tag for the white hen. But there was a Kansas trip on the schedule, and a week passed before I made it back to the white hen's stomping grounds. When I did, though, I had no trouble finding her again. She didn't come to the field that day, but I got a conversation going with a pair of gobblers in a deep, wooded hollow behind the pasture, and when they came in She was with them.

I could have killed either or both of these gobblers as they strutted and gobbled in front of me, but I held off on the gobblers for the second time in my life. She was just beyond comfortable range, and I was determined to have this bird in my office. As hard as it is for me to believe, I let those two gobblers walk. She walked with them.

She walked with them again the next day, although this time I wasn't able to call them all the way to the gun. They gobbled 500 times

Bad Birds 2

The pressure was off. Now it was time to concentrate on the white hen.

and gave me a great hunt, but the white hen stubbornly refused to come close enough.

I went out of state again after that, and when I returned there was only one day left in the season. I went to the pasture at daylight, and found it as devoid of turkeys as a tennis court. Nothing gobbled anywhere within hearing, and I circled and criss-crossed the 500 acres of forest surrounding the pasture until noon without hearing or seeing a turkey.

But stubborn is as stubborn does, and I was in it for the long haul. That afternoon, the last day of the season, I went to the pasture at about 3 o'clock, built a blind against a big oak and settled in for the duration.

It was almost sundown when I finally gave it up. My butt was asleep and I'd given it my best shot. I started putting my calls in my vest and gathering the rest of my stuff, and I was just about to get to my feet when I glanced into the field one last time and saw what looked like a white cat, 200 yards out there, moving in and out of the partially-grazed bluestem.

Maybe it looked like a cat, but I knew better. I watched for a little while, and then She raised her head and looked around. Then She started walking my way.

The rest is anti-climactic. When She started veering to the right I yelped one time, to get her back on course. She obligingly made the correction and walked straight at me, and when She was 30 yards away I clucked. She stopped, raised her head, and a few seconds later I was holding her down so She wouldn't mess up her feathers.

And I was right. She looks good in my office.

Bad Birds 2

I was right. She looks good in my office.

17

Br'er Rabbit

It was Saturday, Opening Day, on the long side of midmorning. I'd had an uneventful hunt so far, with only a few distant gobbles. I was prospecting, covering ground, when a gobbler answered my crow call. I was at the edge of an 80-acre clearcut, thick with blackberry, smilax, poison ivy, wild plum and other unpleasant vegetation, so I assumed the gobbler was on the other side. I hotfooted it around the perimeter of the thicket and made another crow call when I got to the back side.

The turkey answered again. It sounded like he was across the clearcut again, about where I'd been when I first heard him. So I went back around, stopped just before I got to my original calling spot, and hit him again. He gobbled, and I figured it out. He wasn't on the other side of the thicket. Rather, he was right out there in the big middle of it.

Well, I thought, *he had to get out there somehow. There's gotta be a road leading in.*

I circled again, but the opposite direction. When I reached the spot on the other side where I'd been earlier, I'd completely circled the thicket and still hadn't found an entrance.

By now the turkey was gobbling on his own. Not a lot, but every two or three minutes. Back then, my hunting mantra was "If I can hear him, I can get to him," so I picked a marginally thinner section of brush and waded in. A peppy snail could have made better time than I did in that awful place. I tried my best to be quiet, but it was wasted

Br'er Rabbit didn't much like being in the open. He wanted a thicket close by at all times.

effort. In ten minutes I covered maybe 100 yards, and I wouldn't have been much noisier if I'd been a rhino. Predictably, the gobbler heard me coming and dummied up. I sat on a pine stump and waited 30 minutes, but when he didn't start talking again I decided to leave. That's when I discovered I'd lost my compass, and this was a couple decades before GPS, smart phones, On X Hunt, Huntstand, US Topo Maps or any of those wussy devices and apps we use today. We had three choices back then: have an intimate knowledge of the land, use a compass, or be skilled at dead reckoning.

Maybe you can dead-reckon your way out of a dog-hair thicket when the sun is straight up and obscured by heavy cloud cover to boot. Not me. I plowed around in that hell-hole for two hours before finally emerging, looking like I'd been fighting wildcats.

During that ordeal, though, I found the gobbler's holding spot. Found it three times, in fact, and from a different direction each time.

Br'er Rabbit

It was a gladey, rocky arena almost as big as a football field, but when I finally found my way out of there, I still didn't know how to get back to his sweet spot.

The next morning I was listening at the edge of the clearcut. Nothing. At seven o'clock a distant gobbler finally pulled me away, but I hadn't reached that bird yet when Br'er Rabbit cranked up behind me, again in the middle of the clearcut.

I went to the other gobbler anyway, and in short order he gave me a drubbing and left. Meanwhile, Br'er Rabbit was still gobbling from the fastness of his thicket, and I tried him again.

Entering the thicket, I had a stroke of good fortune. I found my compass hanging from a plum bush. That was the extent of the good stuff, though, and Br'er Rabbit again shut up when he heard me coming. This time, I gave him two hours to start gobbling. No soap.

The next weekend I was back. This time Br'er Rabbit played the part of Tarbaby: He didn't say nothin'.

But neither did any other gobbler within earshot, so I found a comfortable tree within shotgun range of the thicket and settled in. At 2 p.m. I left, not having heard a single gobble. Sunday morning it was raining buckets, and I went back home.

The next weekend I took two days of vacation and was there early Thursday afternoon. Br'er Rabbit was gobbling, and I got a compass line on his glade and made another approach. This time I brought a heavy-duty garden pruner. Though even slower, I was much quieter on approach. I got close enough to see part of the glade, and he was still gobbling. Twenty more yards, and I could just stand there until he ambled into view.

I'd covered ten of the 20 when two does got up underfoot. They ran out across the glade, snorting and blowing like pigs, and Br'er Rabbit knocked off for the day. I stayed until the shadows got long, then went back to camp.

The pathway I'd clipped gave me relatively easy access to the glade, and next morning I went in by flashlight. I hit the clearing at first light, and by gobbling time I'd made a brush blind against a rockpile near one edge of the glade. I just needed to wait.

As it turned out, I also needed to be able to see through rocks. When he gobbled at 9:30, he was directly behind the rockpile, close but hidden. The rocks and my dense blind kept him safe until he skirted the edge of the glade, but by that time he was 60 yards out. I tried to call him back but he couldn't see the hen, and he hadn't gotten old by being foolish. I tried to bend him to my will, but it just made him more suspicious. After 20 minutes he slipped into the brush, and I heard no more from him that day.

Before leaving the glade I rearranged my blind so I could see the place where I believed he'd come into the open. But I guessed wrong. The next day he came in different and was behind me again. I couldn't do anything with him that day, either, and ended up overcalling and blowing him out of the glade again.

The next day, Sunday, I needed to quit by noon. I didn't even take a call with me, but it made no difference. Br'er Rabbit was a no-show.

Not only were electronic aids not available back then, but seasons were also longer in some states. The next two weekends were wash-outs, one literally, the other due to a crisis at work, and the final weekend of the season was at hand. Decision time: keep after Br'er Rabbit, or look for a more biddable gobbler.

By then ego had taken over, and I was drawn to that clearcut like a coon to a cornfield. My blind was still usable, and I crawled into it vowing to stay all day and not make a call. I kept both vows, nobody showed up, and I returned to camp at sundown in a foul mood. Sunday was Saturday's re-run, and at 11 a.m. I told myself I'd give it another hour and call it a season.

At 11:07, Br'er Rabbit gobbled. Seconds later he stepped into view at the far end of the glade. At 2:30, he was still down there, never closer than 60 yards. I couldn't stand it any longer and gave him a string of soft yelps.

He stretched his wrinkled old neck, stood motionless for two minutes, then walked back into the thicket.

18

The Paintball King

From a distance, the mountain looks easy. It towers several hundred feet above its surrounding hills – which for somebody from the Rockies would be laughable, but it's a pretty big deal here in the Ozarks. Anyway, it's taller than its neighbors and you can see it from a long way off, but even with its extra height it looks gentle and rounded and inviting. It's not until you find yourself clambering around on its rock-strewn, deceptively steep slopes that you figure out your earlier assessment was wrong. Sadly wrong.

But a Bad Bird I named The Paintball King lived on the mountain, and so for a week in 2002 I pretty much did, too.

Since it's higher than everything else around it, the mountain sprouts a cluster of microwave, telephone and assorted other relay towers from its noggin, and the three or four acres around these structures has been cleared of timber. Since it's the only clearing on the mountain (the only one I know about, anyway,) it's a draw for deer, turkeys and other wildlife. This is especially so since the road leading to the top is rough and steep and circles the mountain like a section of overstretched screen door spring. There's little traffic except for service vehicles and good old boys drinking beer. And, in the spring, a masochistic turkey hunter or two.

Because of its elevation, the clearing is also a good listening spot. Good, that is, if your sole criterion is being able to hear gobbling turkeys. However, if your goal is to not only hear turkeys but also get to them afterwards, often it's not so good. My mantra as a young(er) turkey hunter was "If I can hear him, I can get to him." This mountain caused me to quit saying that.

I misjudged the amount of time it would take me to drive up that bumpy corkscrew of a road, and there were already three turkeys gobbling when I reached the top that first morning. I wasn't very close to any of them, but the closest bird was racking 'em off at about a gobble every five seconds. It didn't take me long to gather my stuff and drop off the side of the mountain in his direction.

The turkey was on the ground by the time I managed to slip and slide the 400 vertical feet and 900 horizontal ones to get close to him. Although the place he flew down on was fairly flat, it was also a pretty impressive boulder field. With all those big rocks for cover, it would have made a pretty good paintball battleground, and now you know how he got his name. I got within a hundred yards of him and set up with my back against one of those free-standing slabs of rock.

He was gobbling so much it was hard to tell if he was answering me or just gobbling, but every time I called, he gobbled. So, naturally, my conceit as a turkey hunter is that he was, indeed, answering me. Of course, he gobbled eight or ten or twenty times on his own between each of my calls, too, so maybe not.

Whichever, though, he did approach, and as he came I caught a glimpse of him twice between boulders – once at 90 yards, the second time at 50. But then he hung up, within shotgun range but behind a couple big rocks, and that's where he stayed. I was able to use those same rocks for cover while I moved 30 feet to the side and made another set, but he'd made his stand. I couldn't get any more cooperation out of him. He eventually moved away and I fell in behind him, but that strategem worked exactly as well as it usually does – which is to say, not at all. After tagging along behind him for a couple hours, he finally shook me off his back trail about 11 a.m. After another fruitless two hours of trying to raise another gobbler, I made the difficult climb back up the mountain to my truck.

I drove back up there just before sundown and more or less roosted him, and took a compass bearing from the mountaintop. Near as I could tell, he was on the west end of the boulder field, which gave me hope. The next morning I was there much earlier, and used a pen-light to get down the mountain until I figured I was in his neighborhood. Somehow I managed to do it without breaking my neck. Sure enough, he was in a big snag-topped shortleaf pine that grew on the edge of a steep slope hard by the boulder field. And sure as old age follows youth, he flew down into it again.

I was already in there when he did, though, and he very nearly made a bad mistake that second morning. I saw him leave his tree and sail toward me, and if he'd landed just six feet farther west I'd have killed him before he got his feathers adjusted. But he didn't, and for the next 30 minutes he stayed squarely behind the Volkswagen-sized rock he landed behind, while I pointed my gun at the thing and yelped my lips sore. After a while he didn't gobble any more, and if you know where he went I'd appreciate you telling me because I don't have a damn clue. That was Morning Two.

Morning Three, he roosted in more or less the same place, but this time he didn't fly down into the boulder field where I lay in wait. Today he flew farther down the mountain and set up shop, not gobbling as much as he'd been doing the two previous days but still plenty enough to pull me out of the boulder field and down into the hollow with him.

When I got down there with him and yelped, he started a slow march back up the mountain and went into the boulder field again. After I laboriously climbed back up there, we went through another peekaboo session between the rocks before he disappeared. Again.

I rested both him and me the fourth day. On Day Five, he worked me for an hour and a bit, then circled me in the boulders and came in behind. He saw me, putted and left in a great hurry. This was beginning to get old.

Bad Birds 2

The paintball king

A horrendous thunderstorm at daylight on Day Six rested us both again, but by late morning the sun came out and I drove up the mountain to listen. He gobbled at my third crow call, from the middle of the paintball zone. He must have heard me slipping and sliding down the wet mountainside, though, because I never heard him again after I got in there with him. I didn't have anything better to do, so I just made myself comfortable and settled in for the rest of the day.

An hour before sundown he started gobbling at the west end of the boulder field, and I slipped out the east end and circled carefully to the edge of the drop-off that overlooked the trees where he'd been roosting. I set up against a big red oak facing the sound of the gobbling and quietly waited for whatever was going to happen.

The sun was low on the horizon when he showed up. He'd quit gobbling by now and when I first saw him he was walking and pecking, moving along the narrow strip of open woods between the boulder field and the drop-off. He was coming straight at me. When he crossed the 35-yard line, I clucked at him and he stopped and raised his head.

He could have had the courtesy to die right there, but nooooo. Instead, he did the headless-chicken flop off the edge and down the slope for 75 yards until he fetched up against a log, and I had to go down there after him.

I didn't mind all that much.

19

Devil Anse

As rivers go, the Tug Fork isn't such a much. Still, it separates eastern Kentucky from western West Virginia, and it once separated the lands of two feuding families you may have heard about: the Hatfields and the McCoys. The gunsmoke and mayhem from that 28-year feud have long since left the valley of the Tug Fork, and these days most of the gunfire heard in these parts is from deer hunters.

And, in the spring, turkey hunters. The Tug Fork runs through some pretty good turkey country. It was there, not more than three or four miles from the original homestead of clan leader Captain William Anderson (Devil Anse) Hatfield at the mouth of Thacker Creek, that I got acquainted with a gobbler that was every bit as ornery and as resourceful as that feuding old mountain man. What else could I have possibly named him?

Our relationship began in familiar turkey hunting fashion: he came to me fresh off the roost, then hung up at 70 yards. He kept me on the edge of my cushion for nearly an hour, then left me alone in the West Virginia woods. I didn't think much about it at the time. After all, I've grown accustomed over the years to having my inadequate credentials examined by gobblers. I had plenty of time to study him, though, as he strutted and pirouetted for me in the clear, wide open 25 yards beyond shotgun range. It seemed to me he was a little darker than a normal turkey, and though I didn't have any others to compare him against that morning, he seemed a little bigger than your average West Virginia gobbler.

I was back on his ridge at first light the next morning, high above Thacker Creek. Near as I could tell, he was gobbling from the same tree he'd roosted in the day before. I set up a little closer to him this time, pushing my luck, but I got away with it. I heard him flap and thump when he flew down. He came to me again, but this time two other gobblers closed on us from downhill toward the creek.

I'd been right; compared with the other two gobblers he was considerably bigger and darker. He wasted no time in running them off, flogging the gobbler that had enough nerve to challenge him and intimidating the other with aggressive strutting and posturing. I could see he was a force to be reckoned with, and that's when I hung the name on him.

All in all it was a grand show, but again it happened too far off my gun barrel for me to do anything but watch. After it was over, Anse appeared to lose interest in my calling. He continued to strut and he gobbled some, but after a while he went the other way. As soon as I could safely move I got up and tried to get around him and set up in his path, but that worked as well as it usually does. I stayed on the ridge until the 1 p.m. closing time without hearing any turkey noises whatsoever.

The next morning he was henned up, but far enough from them on the roost that I was able to get in between and spook the hens off the side of the ridge. Devil Anse had been gobbling fairly steadily, about every 45 seconds, but predictably he shut up when I flushed all his hens. I dug in and waited for him to do something, but it was as though the earth had swallowed him up.

Finally, at 8 a.m., I saw him sail silently from the direction of his roost tree and execute that herky-jerky, semi-controlled crash landing big gobblers generally make. He was nearly in gun range when he touched down, and when everything got quiet after his landing I waited until he relaxed out of alert posture and then clucked softly, one time, with a mouth call. He jerked alert again, stood still for ten seconds, then took three steps to his left, my right, and went behind a big red oak. It gave me the chance to get my gun up and I did, but I might as well have left it in the truck. He didn't come out from behind that tree until he was 80 yards away, and then he was walking purposefully in the opposite direction.

I normally don't roost turkeys because I consider it largely a waste of effort, but time was running out and I was due in Pennsylvania in two more days. That evening I was on the ridge with him and heard him fly up, into the same group of trees he'd roosted in the last three nights. I was pretty sure I knew where he'd flown up from, too, and with the aid of a green penlight and a little blind luck, I found the place 30 minutes before first light the next morning.

When gobbling time came, Devil Anse started up right on cue. I sat tight and let him gobble, and even though the hens I'd run off the previous morning had reassembled, they were behind me when they started tree-yelping.

I never made a sound. I had in mind some half-baked idea about trying to spook the hens if they flew down first and came past me going to him, but I didn't have to try to make it work. I heard them start coming to the ground a hundred yards away, and 15 seconds later Anse left his limb and came sailing straight at me through the trees, his white head looking as big as a softball against the dark feathers. He back-braked and landed noisily 25 yards out, and those two or three herky-jerky post-landing steps big gobblers usually take took him behind another red oak. Up came my gun.

He gobbled behind the tree, and when he did his head came out from behind the trunk. I shifted my gun to the spot and waited. Thirty seconds later he gobbled again, and the head reappeared just above my bead. I adjusted the point of aim and waited.

On the third gobble, the bead was on his head when it came into view around the red oak trunk. When I slapped the trigger, a paint bucket full of bark blew out of the side of the tree, but enough of the

In West Virginia it takes a big gobbler to weigh 23 pounds. That's what Devil Anse weighed.

shot got past it to get the job done. When I got over there, Anse was tearing around in the leaves, making enough racket to wake the original Devil Anse, dead now for well over a century.

In that part of the world, it takes a hell of a big turkey to weigh 23 pounds. That's what this one weighed. He was darker than usual, as I'd thought, due mostly to the deeper-than-average mahogany coloring between the black bars of his tail fan. You had to get the feathers in direct sunlight to be able to tell the black from the brown.

I'll probably never get another chance to hunt the Hatfield clan's ancestral homeland, but in a way I don't really mind. If the other turkeys there are as tough as Devil Anse, I don't have any business hunting them, anyway.

20

Steve Martin

It was late March, the turkeys were already gobbling hard, and Opening Day was still two interminable weeks away. I was doing whatever I could to ward off the pre-season heebie jeebies. Nowadays, with all the kids grown and gone and a little more jingle in my pockets, I load up and head for Alabama, Georgia, Florida or Mississippi. Back then, putting shoes on the feet of a small mob of rug rats, I didn't have two spare nickels to rub together. The travel option was not on the table, so I fought the restlessness by spending a lot of time in the woods, prowling, looking, listening.

I'd found a dependable turkey and was trying to learn as much about him as I could. This particular morning, I'd heard him gobble six or seven times and had moved closer each time. But that last move brought me a little too close, and when he gobbled again he was just out of sight over a little hill. Not wanting to bump him, I hurriedly fell down by a handy tree and yanked my head net and gloves out of my vest.

I'd barely finished suiting up when three hens appeared at 30 yards. A few seconds later I heard the buzz and thump of his drumming and seconds after that the boss himself appeared. He was tucked into a full, gut-straining strut, and he was obviously overcome with his own self-importance.

Regal as he was, though, there was still something odd about the way he looked. Instead of dropping his wing tips toward the ground in the typical leaf-raking posture of a strutting gobbler, this one sort of flopped his wings out sideways and down. It reminded me of the way a female killdeer fakes a broken wing to lure you away from its nest or babies. Where most strutting gobblers look like a round, fuzzy featherball, this one had a sort of notch in his back where the feathers weren't fully raised, and he appeared to be balancing a stick on his back.

At first, I didn't understand what I was looking at. But when he turned sideways I could see orange and yellow fletching against his dark back feathers, and I figured it out: the gobbler had been wounded by a bow hunter, and the arrow was still stuck through his body. It took him high on the back, it looked like, from right to left about halfway between his neck and his tail, and there was about ten inches of the shaft sticking out on each side. The fletching was still there, but as far as I could tell the broadhead had broken off.

I have no idea why the arrow didn't pass on through, and how the gobbler had survived the wound I can't even begin to imagine, but bow season had ended more than three weeks earlier and here he was. No surprise, he didn't look as healthy as he would have been otherwise, but he obviously had love on the brain and was doing the best he could. I watched him, bug-eyed as a kid at a circus, until he followed the hens on down the hillside and out of sight. He gobbled three times while I was watching him, and each time he nearly fell over but staggered around and kept his feet under him.

It was an amazing performance, and by the time he was out of sight I'd already named him after the 1970s-80s-and 90s stand-up comedian whose running gag was the fake arrow sticking through his head. I also set a goal: I was going to kill this arrow-toting gobbler, and kids' shoes be damned, I was going to have a full body mount done, arrow and all.

I saw him once more before the season opened, when I got in close at daylight and watched him fly down into a food plot. He flew as effortlessly as a normal gobbler; it was only after he hit the ground and tried to strut that he favored the wound. My admiration for him grew, as did my desire to kill him.

Opening Day found me in Steve Martin's neighborhood, listening to him rattle the woods from his roost. But in my eagerness I pushed him a little. I don't think he saw me, but he heard me, and it made him dummy up. He flew down the other way, and I never heard him gobble again that morning.

The second morning I altered my strategy. I'd scouted him so thoroughly I pretty well knew where he'd be at midmorning, so I left him gobbling on the roost and set up on the hill where I'd seen him the first time. My plan was to wait him out and shoot him when he came through. It was working, and he was steadily approaching when another hunter came in from the other way and started hammering at him with a cacophony of yelps, cutts and cackles. Steve didn't go to the second hunter, but the loud, incessant calling made him alter his line of travel. He went by me in the bottom of the hollow rather than on the hilltop where I waited. The woods were open as a city park and I saw him go by at 150 yards.

When he was out of sight I took rounders and tried to get ahead of him again, but it didn't work and day two ended like Opening Day.

The weekend died and I had to go back to work, but Wednesday I played hooky and was out there again. Steve Martin was gobbling. I was again on the hilltop with him and had him coming, and I was feeling cocky about the whole thing when something happened on the other side of the hill. There was some clucking and putting, a frantic scuffling of leaves, and turkeys flew out in several directions. One of them was Steve; I could clearly see the yellow fletching as he sailed out over the valley. A minute or so later, a coyote topped the hill 75 yards away, looking hungry.

After two more long days in the office, I was back on Steve's hilltop. Unfortunately, so was a big thundercloud. It rained both days of the weekend, and although I hunted all morning both days and got as wet as a snapping turtle, I never heard a turkey and never saw a feather.

The rain continued through most of the week, but the skies cleared Wednesday afternoon and I made arrangements to be off Thursday and Friday. Thursday morning I was between Steve's roost area and the hilltop where he liked to strut, and when he flew down I let him gobble twice on his own and then yelped sharply, cutting into the back side of his gobble. He answered me immediately and three minutes later he was there, wings splayed comically, yellow fletching gleaming in the sun.

I let him come, and at 25 yards decided it was time to end the show. Your guess is as good as mine how I missed him. Maybe my head wasn't down on the gun. Maybe I was looking at that yellow fletching and shot at it instead of his head. Maybe I hit him where I was supposed to, and he was just plain unkillable. He was, after all, carrying that arrow around like a living pincushion.

Whatever the story, he flew off the hilltop and the season closed the next day and I never saw him again.

Steve Martin, doing a stand-up act with a cheesy, familiar, hilarious prop.

21

Ringo

Most turkeys are aggravating, but Ringo took the prize. I really can't tell you why I hunted him as much as I did, except that I was still far down the learning curve and hadn't yet learned the best thing to do with some gobblers is walk away from them. It was a year when conditions were right and gobblers were plentiful, and most of the mornings I hunted him I could hear other turkeys gobbling. Maybe I could have killed one of those other birds, and today, nearly 40 years later, I know I'd have at least tried. But I'll never know about the killability of those other turkeys, because I couldn't drag myself away from this old boy.

The thing is, Ringo was so findable. He roosted every night in a patch of hardwood timber on the point of a ridge, between a rough three-year-old clearcut and a mature stand of shortleaf pine. He never chose the same tree, but he'd always be close. And he'd gobble like clockwork, starting at that stage of breaking day when you can see branches against the sky but not what's underfoot.

The problem was, he didn't gobble much – five or six times, always spaced far enough apart to give me time to get reasonably close and set up. But then he'd fly down and dummy up. I hunted him seven times that spring, and in that week's worth of hunting I heard him gobble a total of five times after his feet hit the ground.

Which is not to say he was hard to keep track of after he flew down. He'd either pitch down into the big pines, where the forest floor was as clean of understory as a Pebble Beach fairway, or he'd drop pretty much straight off his limb and either stay in the hardwoods or wander into the clearcut. Either way, my set-up was always close enough that I could see him leave the limb and usually see him for a while after he was on the ground.

My ears were still in pretty good shape then, and I could easily hear a turkey drum at well over a hundred yards. Even farther, if it was a good, still morning and the gobbler was leaning into it a little. And Ringo really leaned into it. He droned nonstop for two to three hours every morning, and the buzz and thump from his chest let me know he was still there even when I didn't have him in sight. That's how he earned his name, after Ringo Starr. Drummer, get it?

Ringo would drum for me all morning, but he simply wouldn't come. When he was in the pines, he never got closer than 60 yards, and I now know now it was because he could see too well that he wouldn't close the gap. The hen should have been visible, and he knew it. She never was, so he never came in.

When he was in the clearcut, Ringo would sometimes come closer, but the briars and bunch grasses were thick out there where the trees used to be. I couldn't see more than 20 yards into the stuff, and he never got that close. Sometime during the midmorning he'd grow tired of drumming at an invisible hen and wander off to wherever he spent the middle part of the day. Since he gobbled so infrequently, I never figured out where that was.

I tried several different strategies, none of which worked. Three mornings I got into the pines in an effort to be there when he flew down, but each time he went into the clearcut. Three mornings I set up in the hardwoods as close as I could get to his roost tree, and each of those times he sailed into the pines. I even tried double-teaming him, taking a buddy and one of us setting up in each location. That morning, he flew directly into the clearcut. It was the only time I ever saw him do that.

I even tried a decoy one morning. They were just coming into

Ringo was practically unkillable, but on the last afternoon of the season, he made a mistake.

vogue, and the one I had was hard-bodied, shaped like an egg, and favored a penguin more than a turkey. Ringo acted predictably when he saw it: he slicked down, stood at suspicious attention for three full minutes, then turned his back and marched into the clearcut, where he resumed his drum solo.

The last day of the season that year, I decided to try him in the afternoon. I slipped onto the ridge at 3 o'clock and stuck a leafy-branch blind in front of a big red oak on the border between the pines and Ringo's hardwood roosting area. At 5:30 I woke from a nap to the unmistakable sound of Ringo's signature song.

Drumming is ventriloquistic at best, and when a hunter is groggy from a nap it's even more so. Not knowing its direction, though, didn't disguise the fact that its origin was very close. First, I raked my eyes as far left and right as the eyeball muscles would permit. Nothing. V-e-r-y s-l-o-w-l-y, I turned my head left, farther left, farther left. At the very limit of my peripheral vision, with my head turned as far that way as it could go without breaking my neck, I saw a blurry black blob with a smaller white blob in the center of it. The range was approximately 15 yards.

It was an impossible situation. I shoot off my left shoulder, and though I've killed a dozen or so gobblers off my right side, he was simply too close to risk any movement at all. As slowly as before, I moved my head back to a less agonizing position and sat still. The drumming continued, now louder, now softer. It was almost 7 o'clock when I caught a flash of black, this time out of the corner of my right eye. Slowly, Ringo came into sharper focus as he shuffled his way forward. This time he was about 25 yards off the gun, directly in front.

When he was in proper position, he obligingly turned his big, beautiful tail fan toward me. Even semi-novice turkey hunters know that's the time to make the move, and when he twirled back around he was staring down the barrel of my 870. A sharp cluck on my mouth call made him run his head up, and I swear in the instant before I

pulled the trigger I saw in his eyes the look of defeat.
　　That's the way I remember it, anyway. And since it's my story, that's the way I tell it.

Bad Birds 2

22

Blinky

I'd only been hunting turkeys seven or eight years when I met the turkey I eventually named Blinky.

He lived on an unusual land feature for the Ouachita Mountains – a steep-sided ridge shaped like a New Mexico mesa, maybe 600 feet above the surrounding terrain. The sides of this thing weren't quite vertical, but still were steep enough that you needed both hands and both feet to climb it. Once you got up there, though, it was flat as a football field, about 200 yards wide and 600 yards long, well-timbered with a mixed stand of oak, hickory and shortleaf pine. There was some groundline vegetation, huckleberries and such, but not much of it.

In other words, it was a good place for a gobbler to strut and show off his fine self, and this old turkey thought it was just peachy. I first heard him on a drive-and-scout expedition three days before the turkey season opener. I was on a Forest Service road that ran along the base of the ridge's south side. Because of the distance to the top and the fact that he wasn't close to the edge – and also because years of unprotected shooting have taken their toll on my eardrums – I could just barely hear him. It was a workday and already well past sunrise, and I could tell from eyeballing the steep slope I didn't have time to get up there to him to pinpoint his location. So I listened to him for a while and drove back to town.

That was a Wednesday. Thursday I stopped at the same spot on the road below the mesa and heard him again, up there on top. Ditto Friday. Guess where I was at first light on Saturday, Opening Day?

If you've never climbed a cow-face slope made of shale and loose chunk rock in the dark with a shotgun slung across your chest and a Mini Mag light in your mouth, let me give you some heartfelt advice: *Keep it that way.* Somehow I made it to the top without performing a Humpty Dumpty, and when I finally got up there I even had time to catch my breath and ease my cramping fingers and forearms before gobbling time.

Since I'd never been on the mesa before and didn't know where he roosted (if he roosted up there at all,) I didn't want to risk moving around on the flat until I knew more about the situation. Even though I was a relative newcomer to turkey hunting, I'd still bumped quite a few gobblers by blundering under their roost trees in the near-dark. So I eased to the base of the nearest tree, leaned my gun against the scaly bark, and sat down to wait for gobbling time.

Plop! Plop-plop! The first plop was right beside me on the pine needles. The second was on the bill of my cap and my left shoulder. Exploring fingers revealed the awful truth: turkey turds. As the light grew (interminably slowly) and the woods began to wake up, so did the gobbler's bowels directly overhead. He bombed me twice more in the next 30 minutes, and then he started gobbling. By rolling my head to the side I could peer into the tree and see him, 15 yards above, and I could have rolled him off the limb any time I wanted.

But even back then I didn't want to kill turkeys that way – not even turkeys that had so egregiously disrespected me like this one had. I was too close to him to do any calling, so I just sat there amongst the turkey turds and waited. And waited some more.

Finally he flew down, gliding silently through the big timber and landing barely in sight at about 90 yards. He immediately went into strut with his tail toward me, and I took the opportunity to wipe the biggest part of his anal excreta off myself. Then I eased my gun down from its leaning place against the tree, slid a diaphragm call onto my tongue, and answered him the next time he gobbled.

I've never had much luck calling a gobbler back to the vicinity of his roost tree, and my luck ran true to form that morning. He turned around, looked my way and gobbled a few times, but when he started moving it wasn't in my direction. I let him get out of sight and then angled his way, using the break of the slope to hide my advance.

It was a typical, frustrating, unsuccessful morning. He strolled around on his flat mountaintop, gobbling at my calls, at crows, at blue jays and at anything else that struck his fancy, and after a while he shut up and I lost track of him. I stayed up there until the middle of the day, but I never heard him gobble after 8 o'clock. Flicking dried remnants of turkey poop off my clothes, I descended the slope faster but with no less difficulty than I'd climbed it six hours earlier.

Sunday morning I climbed the ridge 200 yards farther north, in case he was roosted in the same vicinity. He was, and it sounded like he was in the same tree. I closed the distance in the gloaming and set up as close as I could to where he'd pitched down the morning before. Naturally, he flew out the other way. I followed and we played a repeat of Saturday's hunt. But at least this time I didn't go home smelling like the floor of a turkey house.

Arkansas had a 37-day turkey season in those days and this was before I became a traveling turkey hunter, so this mountaintop bird became my project for the season. You know how it is; a bird gets inside your head, and nothing seems as important as killing him. In the decades since, I've figured out the best thing to do is write off birds like this, but I didn't know it then.

So I wasted a goodly portion of that season trying to kill an unkillable turkey. Unkillable by me, at least. I didn't go to him on every hunt, but I went to him often enough. I made contact every single time I went up there, saw him three or four times, but never got him any closer than 60 yards. I tried using a decoy, I tried building a brush blind, I tried stalk-and-bushwhack. The season ended with him still strolling around on top of the mesa and me grinding my teeth.

Opening Day the next year I was on the mesa again. I'd heard him up there on two scouting mornings, but hadn't climbed to the top. But I was waiting for him to open up on the first morning of the season, and he didn't disappoint. He was 150 yards away, and as I closed the distance I came to small patch of windthrown trees that had come down sometime during the off season. There were five or six of them, scattered over about an acre, and I found a comfortable spot against one of the root balls.

The gobbler seemed more interested this time, and when he hit the ground he headed my way. I saw him at 80 yards when he came through a gap between two big oaks, and then he slipped behind one of the blowdowns. The next time I saw him, he was 25 yards off the gun barrel. He was on the other side of the blowdown that had hidden his approach, and he was looking at me through a saucer-sized hole in the branches. I already had the gun shouldered and ready and pointed in the right direction, and I could have shot through his peephole and busted him right then. But I wanted to see him him in the open, so I waited.

It was a standoff. His black, shiny eye was centered in the hole, his white head as big as a softball. I was a wreck, trembling like a sick dog. I remember thinking: *Be still. Be Calm. Wait him out. Don't do anything stupid.*

And then, of course, I did something stupid.

It never occurred to me that if I could see his eyeball through that hole, he could see mine as well. But he could, and when I blinked, things went sideways in a hurry. The gobbler couldn't have reacted more violently if I'd hit him with a cattle prod. He was airborne in a tenth of a second, and although I could have blown him out of the air when he cleared the top of the blowdown at point-blank range, I was too flabbergasted to pull the trigger.

He sailed over the edge of the ridge and out over the road far below, and from my seat against my fallen tree I watched him sail

Blinky

across a wide valley and land on the slope of another ridge a thousand yards away. All I could think of to do was shake my head and grin.

I climbed up there three more times during the course of that season, but I never saw or heard that turkey again. And now you know why I named him Blinky.

Don't move a muscle. Not even your eyelids.

Bad Birds 2

23

The Lineman

He was Jill's turkey. I'd been coming in second with another gobbler across the highway and two miles south of where my wife was fighting her own losing battle with this one.

Her Bad Bird headquartered in a pair of small but steep-sided hollows that topped out at the edge of the blacktop road and ran half a mile gently downslope before leveling out into a flat, brushy cut-over. Less than 75 yards from the highway, two high-voltage power line rights of way crossed the twin hollows, paralleling the highway and about 100 yards apart. A pretty stand of mature timber separated them.

The Lineman always roosted in the head of one of the hollows between the blacktop and the power lines, but he was quiet in the evenings. Jill never knew which hollow he was roosted in until he gobbled in the morning. He was so close to the highway there was no way to set up above him, and there was so little maneuvering room between the power lines and the highway it was too risky to set up in there with him. So she had to start each hunt downhill from her bird, and on the wrong side of a 50-yard-wide right of way to boot.

Not a high percentage situation. She'd wait on the ridge between the hollows until he gobbled, then get on the slope of whichever hollow he was roosted in and wait for him to fly down. But The Lineman had too many options, and he was a wise old bird besides. He'd cross into the other hollow and go downhill behind her to the power line, or he'd come out in the first power line before he got to her. He'd always go one way or another on one of the two rights of way, though, except for the one morning he crossed the blacktop onto land she didn't have permission to hunt.

He was a frustrating turkey, but he gobbled so much he was fun to hunt. And as frustrating turkeys often do, he got under Jill's skin.

After four days of consecutive drubbings, I took a break from my bird. Jill wasn't ready to take a break from hers, so we decided to try double-teaming him. We split up to cover both roosting hollows, and went in early enough to get into the narrow roosting strip between the power lines and the highway.

And so, naturally, he wasn't roosting there that time. When he cranked up, he was in the strip of big timber between the power lines. He was in Jill's hollow, but by the time he started gobbling there was already too much light for her to cross the open area and get in there with him. I could get over there, though because I had the ridge to hide behind. I hot-footed it down my hollow and across the first power line, then eased as far up the slope toward The Lineman's hollow as I figured I could get away with.

My set-up couldn't have been much more than 50 yards from him, but I might as well have been on Saturn's 57th moon for all the good it did me. He gobbled back hard and angry at my first call, then gobbled again on his own a minute later and considerably farther away. The next time I heard from him, he was heading west along the second power line, apparently with a destination in mind and a powerful need to get there. I couldn't catch up to him before he left the property.

The next morning we tried a different strategy. Jill went in close, above the power lines and into the woods beside the highway. I set up in the other hollow but stayed back, setting up between the power lines. When he started gobbling, Jill was sitting against his roost tree.

"I guess I could have shot him out of the tree," she told me later, "but where's the fun in that?" So she sat and listened to him gobble. At least she didn't get crapped on, the way Blinky did to me in Chapter 22.

The Lineman eventually pitched out, landing within Jill's sight but too far for a shot, and after gobbling some at my distant calling he wandered off west down the uphill power line.

On Day 7, he didn't gobble. Hoping he'd been killed by someone else or maybe eaten by a bobcat, I suggested to Jill we forget about him for a while and hunt elsewhere. We got lucky later that morning and each killed a bird, and after trying unsuccessfully for my Bad Bird the next morning, we returned to try The Lineman again.

Same plan: one of us in each hollow, Jill in tight and me hanging back. But this time he was downhill from both power lines, almost to where the twin hollows merged and played out into the flat cutover. By the time we got to him he was on the ground and out in the thick stuff. We tried to get in there with him, but it was an impossible situation and we backed out rather than run the risk of spooking him.

Jill now had a week of her life invested in this bird, and so far I'd given him three days of mine. I'm all for a challenge – after all, turkey hunting *is* supposed to be tough – but I'm also for killing a turkey every once in a while. I washed my hands of the whole thing and went in search of a more biddable gobbler. Two days later I found one, and my home-state turkey season was over.

Meanwhile, Jill had given The Lineman two more days, and though she saw him both mornings, nothing came of it. I went with her one final morning, we got our butts handed to us again, and then it was time to hit the road. Missouri was calling, and beyond it Ohio, West Virginia and Minnesota.

Jill talked about her unforgettable adversary all the rest of the season, and the longbeards we killed in those other states didn't quench the fire in her belly put there by the one she couldn't kill in Arkansas. She's talked about him off and on through the summer, fall and winter, too. I'd bet a thousand dollars against a used Kleenex I know where my wife is going to be on Opening Day next year.

Look out, Lineman. Jill's a-comin'.

Bad Birds 2

Opening Day came and so did Jill, but The Lineman failed to look out. He walked into a swarm of TSS 9s not long after fly-down time.

24

The Sundance Kid

Never mind that he was a Merriam's gobbler, and Merriam's gobblers are supposed to be easy. Never mind that he lived almost inside the city limits, and heard (and saw) humans, automobiles, dogs and school buses virtually every day of his life. Semi-suburban or not, Merriam's or not, he was one of the toughest turkeys I've ever hunted.

His home range was bisected by a fence separating the Black Hills National Forest from a quarter-mile-wide strip of private land. On the other side of the narrow strip of private was the town of Sundance, Wyoming, which more than a century ago had served as temporary headquarters for a bandit named Harry Longabaugh, who came to be known as the Sundance Kid. You tell me: what else could I have named this particular Bad Bird?

Anyway, he lived partly on the national forest land and partly on the private land, and I suspect he went into a few back yards in town as well. We could hunt the public land, of course, but the private was conspicuously and obnoxiously posted with crude, hand-lettered signs threatening bodily harm to any who dared enter.

Naturally, Sundance spent much of his time behind those signs, gobbling up a storm, while I sat against a ponderosa trunk on the public side of the fence, trying without success to get him to come back out of there.

But he didn't spend all of his time on the private land. He always roosted on the public, and that's where I found him the first morning of our six-day hunt. As is often the case, Jill and I were hunting land we'd never seen before. We walked more than a mile in on a gated road, then split up when the road forked. I hadn't gone far before bumping a hen off the roost, directly above the road I was walking. When she cackled and flew, a nearby turkey rattled out his first gobble of the day. He was close but not alarmingly so, and I found a comfortable set-up and got ready for the hunt.

Since he'd gobbled at the hen I didn't think he needed much more, but I wanted him to know I was still in the vicinity. One set of tree yelps did it. He double-gobbled at the sound, and then set up a steady rhythm of gobbling every 20 seconds until it was light enough for him to fly down. But instead of coming along the road to me like I expected him to do, he went the other way along the road, toward the private land. I followed him until he crossed the fence at a padlocked gate. He continued to gobble in there on the private land for the next two hours, and I finally gave up on him and went looking for another bird.

Didn't find one, though, so after putting him to bed that evening in about the same place I'd found him that morning, I laid a revised plan for the next day's hunt. Getting there a half-hour earlier, I went past the turkey's roost area in the dark and set up within shotgun range of the gate where he'd crossed onto private land the previous day.

He gobbled. He flew down. He came. He veered off the far side of the road before he was killable and went past the crude, rude signs onto the private, in full view in the open ponderosas but 85 yards off my gun barrel. Once again he dropped anchor on his favored gobbling spot, hard against the Sundance city limits, and I left him two hours and 200 gobbles later.

I vowed to forget about him the next morning, but I couldn't find any other birds that wanted to play, so you know how that vow turned out. I did enlist Jill that third day, though, and we got in there early in the afternoon and set up on either side of the road where it entered the posted land, each of us 40 yards from the gate.

Our plan was to bushwhack him on his way back to roost. It's not my favorite way to kill a gobbler, but there are limits on how much crap I'll take from a turkey. Especially on a five-day hunt. We heard him gobble a dozen times down there toward Sundance through the waning hours of the day, and the last couple times he gobbled he was close enough to make us get our guns up and start looking for movement. *Aha,* I thought. *This is going to work.*

But it didn't. He got past us somehow, and at sundown we heard him gobble twice from behind us, 200 yards away in the vicinity of his regular roost. Then we heard his heavy wingbeats, two more gobbles, then nothing. We had to wait until full-on darkness, after which we slipped past him and went back to town.

We slipped past him in the opposite direction the next morning, and at first light we were in the same respective set-ups we'd used the day before, each of us 40 yards from the padlocked gate. He started gobbling on cue. He flew down. He walked the road toward us. We both saw him at 125 yards as he approached, and we both eased our guns up and waited. I don't know about Jill, but I was feeling pretty dang smug.

Just before he got to where we could kill him, he stopped. For a timed 75 minutes, which at the time seemed like 75 hours, he strutted on that two-track road 55 yards from both of us. He was in full sight the whole time, and we were pinned down like bugs on a corkboard. He refused to come a foot closer. Then a hen yelped behind him and he strutted back that way, away from the private land. He found the hen and shut up. We lost contact and didn't hear him again that day.

It being May and it being Wyoming, we woke the next morning to gusting winds laden with what weathermen like to call "winter mix" – that disgusting, hope-draining combination of rain, snow and sleet that makes turkey hunters want to sell all their gear and take up golf. We didn't do that, of course, but we did turn off the alarm and burrow back under the covers. It was 9:30 before conditions improved enough for us to get out there.

Turkeys, though, don't have the option of staying under the covers, and the Kid was in full cry when we arrived. It didn't do us any good, though, and when he left us and entered the private land the way he'd done the first two days, Jill swore off him forever.

The weather continued to improve, and late that afternoon Jill killed a 20-pound bird on private land belonging to a very nice man we'd run into at a Sundance restaurant at noon. She slept in the next morning and I went out to challenge the Kid one more time before leaving for Nebraska. More weather had moved in during the night, and although there wasn't any winter mix in it, the day was still cold and blustery. Not exactly what you'd order up for a turkey hunt.

I felt more like a duck hunter than a turkey hunter as I walked the road toward the posted land. I was cold, discouraged and disgusted, and I was already thinking about the warm truck cab and the 300-mile pull to Valentine.

My train of thought, not to mention my dark mood, changed in a hurry. When he gobbled the first time, he was 80 yards away and still on the limb. I got beside a handy ponderosa, remained standing and braced my gun on the tree. I gave one sharp, brief fly-down cackle and slapped my hat against my leg. He triple-gobbled, and five seconds later I heard the racket he made as he left the tree. When he touched down he was 32 yards off the gun barrel.

Unlike the scene in the movie where Butch and Sundance got shot to pieces by what looked like the entire Bolivian army, I only pulled the trigger once.

It was enough.

The Sundance Kid

After being a true Bad Bird for five days, Butch was a pushover on the sixth.

25

The Sherpa of Matney Mountain

The ancient hump of limestone, granite and dirt they call Matney Mountain has very little flat ground, but it has always had turkeys. And in 2013, one of them gave me a workout. The mountain is the tallest piece of ground in 5,000 square miles. From 50 miles away, maybe more, you can see Matney's dark bulk rising above its lesser neighbors, looming ominously above White River.

I first heard this turkey in early March, while drift-fishing for trout in the river below. Matney's western slope towers over the river, and it's steep as a roofer's ladder. Looking up from the boat to where the turkey was gobbling would give you a sore neck if you did it very long.

I fished that stretch of river four mornings over the next two weeks, and every morning I heard him gobbling from about the same place – on or close to a narrow, 200-yard-long bench far above the river. From below, and keeping the roofing simile alive a little bit longer, the bench looked like a rain gutter strung along the face of the mountains.

The bench was 600 feet above the river, and climbing to him was out of the question. But there's a road across the top of the mountain, and with the help of Google Earth and a topo map I figured out a possible way to get to him. Three days before the season, I made an on-foot scouting trip and confirmed it. It wasn't easy, but I could get in there, and on that trip I heard him gobbling from that narrow bench.

By first light of Opening Day I was just above the south end of that bench. I'd originally planned to use the middle of the bench as my starting point, but decided against it because I didn't know where he liked to roost. That morning, it turned out, he'd slept in a tree 15 feet behind where I stood. I learned this fact in startling fashion.

I like to let turkeys start gobbling on their own, and only resort to trickery if nobody cranks up in a reasonable time. One bird woke up across the river, unreachable and distant, but the bird I was after didn't say anything. So I owled, using that *Hooo-awwww!* scream barred owls often clear their throats with, and the gobbler busted out of that tree behind me like only a spooked gobbler can. He flew directly over my head, low enough to hit with a fishing pole, and scared me so bad I almost fell off the mountain. As I waited for my heart to come back down out of my throat, I watched him sail away down the slope and land on a narrow spit of land right on the bank of the river.

Going down that steep slope was as much out of the question as climbing it had been, so after staying long enough to determine there were no other talky gobblers near the bench, I made the long hike out of there and hunted elsewhere the rest of that day. Late that afternoon I floated past Matney again. My excuse was fishing, but really I was just listening for the turkey, and anything I caught was a bonus. Sure enough, he'd made his way back up to the bench. He didn't gobble much, but he was there.

The next morning, so was I. I detoured around the place where I'd spooked him the day before, and when he started gobbling I was 50 yards above the north end of the bench and he was 50 yards below the south end of it. I quickly moved down close to my end, and by the time I got there I could hear hens tree-yelping between us. Not good, but the terrain surrounding the bench was so steep I figured the flock would at least spend a little time on the flat ground. I set up 10 feet upslope from the bench, my back against a big post oak and my feet against a big rock to keep myself from sliding downhill. It wasn't a comfortable set, but it was the best I could do.

It didn't work. The hens pitched out in the gobbler's direction and he flew down to meet them. They got together 150 yards from me and immediately left the bench going straight uphill. He answered my calls, but the hens pulled him steadily away. I climbed the steep slope flanking them, and somewhere during that difficult hour of climbing and clambering, I started thinking of him as the Sherpa. After that hour of frequent gobbling he abruptly shut up, and I stayed in there for another hour but couldn't raise him again. It was just as well; that laborious hour of trying to stay with the flock just about did me in, and I couldn't have kept it up much longer even if he hadn't quit gobbling. Matney is a far, far cry from Everest, but while I was dragging my worn-out old carcass back to the truck, I officially hung the name on him: Sherpa.

The third day of hunting this turkey was also fruitless. I was at the midway point of the bench at daylight, and he gobbled from his usual position close to the south end. This time I was between the Sherpa and his hens, in what is commonly known as "the catbird seat." They flew down behind me and I gave them enough motion that they got nervous and moved off in the other direction while the longbeard was still in the tree.

Piece of cake, I thought.

And it would have been, if the Sherpa had played fair. Expecting the hens to come to him, he gobbled in the tree well past normal flydown time. Somehow I managed to stay quiet. I didn't hear or see him come down, but when he gobbled on the ground I saw his white head pop out from behind a tree far down the bench. I hit him with a short, excited yelp and his head popped out again when he gobbled, and then he slowly started my way.

He closed the gap to 70 yards and hung up. After gobbling and strutting in place for 20 minutes, he dropped off the flat on the downhill side, went past me under the lip of the bench and came back up there with me. Problem was, he was at that point more than 50 yards off the muzzle. I'd taken the opportunity to reposition while he was out of sight, and had the gun on him, but he was too far and I held off.

He gobbled at me a while, then left going uphill. I flanked him again, climbing with him. I kept up for a while, but he hit some stuff so steep I couldn't handle it. Once again I returned to the truck worn out and empty-handed.

I rested both him and me the next two days, hunting gentler terrain, and managed to kill a nice gobbler the second morning of that rest. I had three more days to hunt close to home before leaving on a long out-of-state turkey safari. I vowed to devote them to hunting the Sherpa of Matney Mountain.

Lacking a better plan, I got on the bench again the next morning. But this time I went in 30 minutes earlier and used the time to sneak into good shotgun range of the south end of the bench. If he flew down like he'd been doing, I was in a position to do something about it.

So of course he broke pattern. The hens were roosted a quarter-mile farther south, on the steep slope of the mountain, and he flew in their direction. I followed, and another morning of climbing the cow's face ensued. I lost them at nine o'clock. That was Sherpa Day Four.

Sherpa Day Five: South end of the bench again. Gobbler roosted uphill this time, but within 50 yards. Hens midway along the bench; I'd evidently sneaked underneath them in the dark. The Sherpa flew down onto the bench, 60 yards from me and 60 yards from the hens. They also flew down. Guess which way he went? When they started uphill, I flanked them again until they hit that same steep area that had defeated me on the third day. This stuff was getting really old.

I almost went elsewhere the last day. I'm glad I didn't. The hens were midway on the bench, in their usual roosting area. He was slightly downhill on the south end of the bench. I came in from uphill on the south end and set up so I could cover the normal landing zone.

Occasionally the turkey gods smile. The Sherpa gobbled a

The Sherpa of Matney Mountain

Piece of cake.

while, and then I heard his hens fly down. A minute later, so did he, and he landed 28 yards away and exactly where I had my gun pointed. I watched him strut for maybe a minute, then clucked sharply.

His head came up.

I filled it with 5s.

Piece of cake.

26

Parker

We'd come to Hawaii for bucket-list purposes, It was a one-and-done, been-there-done-that, got the t-shirt kind of trip. But when you're as eaten up with turkey hunting as Jill and I are, it only made sense to go when turkey season was open on the Big Island. So we went in March.

After spending a day recovering from jet lag and wading through Hawaii's ridiculous gun registration system, we got up fairly early the second morning and made the 50-mile trip from Kona to Waimea to get turkey tags (the Kona Walmart was out of nonresident licenses, don'tcha know.) Good thing we got up early, too. The license-buying ordeal was just as complicated as the gun registration had been, mainly due to a dreary, drawn-out hassle concerning hunter education certifications. But we persevered, and with licenses and gun registrations firmly in hand, we arrived at the public hunting area about 2 p.m.

Through the windshield, the terrain looked like rough traveling as we made a reconnaissance run through part of the area. We soon learned that looks were not deceiving. We were on the west slope of Mauna Kea, nearly two miles above sea level, and the vegetation consisted of wispy, stunted trees and dry, waist-high ground cover that reminded me of tumbleweed except that it stayed put. The stuff wasn't stickery, but that was the best thing you could say about it. Trying to walk through it was like wading through a pond choked with coontail, and to further aggravate the situation, the thick growth hid the solid layer of volcanic chunk rock that littered the ground.

Thank goodness there were places where the stuff didn't grow. When we found one, we got out of the car and walked to the end of a rough two-track that terminated on a knob overlooking the fabled Parker Ranch.

I am pleased to report that the first turkey sound I ever made in Hawaii (a run of yelps on a Ken Morand Longspur Ridge box) produced an immediate gobble. I am not so pleased to report it came from a little stand of trees in a cattle pasture a half-mile into the Parker. The gobbler came out of the trees, little more than a speck of black that far out, and in 90 minutes he cut the distance in half. Meanwhile, we'd moved downhill closer to the boundary, found a decent set-up, and were beginning to get optimistic. That's when everything went sideways.

It had been cloudy all day, but suddenly, very suddenly, it was worse. A dense, cold fog swept across the slope from the north, first blanketing the approaching turkey and then us. Sitting 20 yards apart, Jill and I could barely see one another, and when the fog rolled over the gobbler it shut him down as completely as if somebody had shot him. We sat there another hour, calling without result, and gave it up when the fog started freezing on our gun barrels. Yes, you read that right. We were, after all, above 9,000 feet.

The next morning it was 73 degrees at 4 a.m. in Kona, but by the time we got to the hunting area on Mauna Kea, it was 31 and snowing. (You read that right, too.) But the gobbler was back in his mini-woodlot on the Parker ranch, and again he liked the Morand box. Again he started the long trek across the Parker. But this time he got intercepted by a mob of hens, and that was the end of that. We hunted without success the rest of the morning, and at 2 p.m. we drove off the snowy volcano and back to the warmth of sea level.

It was warmer the third morning, in the 40s at first light, and again the gobbler was talky. But this time, instead of coming closer, he took off more or less parallel to the double boundary fence – web wire on the Parker side, barbed wire three feet from it on the public side. We followed along through the rough, waist-high crap on the public land. He traveled more than two miles, over a ridge and into an area of mixed trees and pasture. The farther he went, the closer he got to the line, but he never got close enough.

He hooked up with several other gobblers in the new place, and they gobbled at us the rest of the day. We quit at 6 p.m. so we'd have time to cover the three miles back to the car before dark.

Our Hawaii trip was more than a turkey hunt, so we took the next few days off to lick our wounds and do touristy things. On our last full day in Hawaii we gave it one more try. By then, Jill was tired of the Parker bird and wanted to hunt lower on the mountain where it was warmer. I dropped her off at about 3,000 feet, where we'd heard gobbling before, and drove on up into snow country. But today it was springtime on the volcano, and the temperature was almost 60. When the cloudless dawn arrived I was near the boundary fence where we'd left the group of gobblers three days earlier.

It reminded me of south Texas – which, I suppose, was appropriate, since Hawaii got its original stock of turkeys from the King Ranch. What sounded like 50 gobblers were trying to out-shout each other, and some were roosted close enough to the property line to give me hope.

Three hours into the morning, that hope was waning. Most of the gobblers had faded farther into the huge ranch, but there were still three birds gobbling less than 300 yards from the line. I found a little ravine that paralleled the double fences and got as close to the turkeys as I could. Over the next hour we engaged in spirited conversation. About ten o'clock I decided to kick it up a notch, since Jill and I had agreed to quit at noon and go see the Kilauea volcano park at the south end of the island. (Six weeks after our visit, Kilauea blew up, but that's another story.)

This one ends on a happier note. I backed off about 50 yards from the fence, got out two vintage push-button Knight & Hale fighting purr calls, laid the Morand box out handy, stuck a raspy diaphragm in my mouth, and for the next two minutes put on the most raucous and lively fight sequence I'm capable of doing.

The three gobblers went nuts. They even got into their own fight over there, and after I finished my own performance I shut up and got ready. I saw the red heads first, bobbing above the brush as they approached the fence at a fast walk. There was a 20-foot-wide bush-hogged right of way along the fence on the ranch side, and when the gobblers reached it they immediately took to the air and cleared both the web-wire and the barbed-wire fences. They landed 35 yards in front of me, and I killed the first one that stuck his head up.

One of the surviving gobblers flew back across the fence, but the third one just stood there. I had another tag and he was legal,

Parker made the decision to fly out of his namesake ranch. It didn't work out well for him.

and there he stood. I had most of the slack pulled out of the trigger when I thought about the two-mile hike back to the vehicle. It would have been tough enough without any turkeys at all. With the one I'd just killed, it was going to be exponentially more difficult. Throw in a second gobbler and it would be murderous.

Anyway, how many kills does it take to let a turkey hunter have bragging rights for the day? Answer: one.

So I kept the barrels of my little Mossberg on his head, yelled *Bang!* at the top of my lungs and watched him fly across the fence to join his buddy.

Was this the same gobbler we'd hunted for three days? I have no idea…but that's what I've been telling everybody. And by the time I finished hauling Parker off that volcano, I was glad I'd passed on filling my second tag.

27

The Gobbler of Heart Attack Mountain

It has an official name, and it's written in a southwest-to-northeast slant on the topo map. I can't remember it any more; it's been nearly two decades since I hunted there. No matter. We called it "Heart Attack Mountain," and that tells you all you need to know.

The flat, spacious top of the mountain was, and no doubt still is, a good place for a gobbler. But it's not a friendly place for a gobbler hunter. Heart Attack isn't particularly tall, only about 500 feet above the surrounding terrain, but every slope leading to that 200-acre plateau is so steep that when you're climbing you can sometimes reach out straight in front of yourself and touch the ground, and in some places the pitch is vertical or even overhanging. As if the steepness wasn't enough, most of the climbable approaches to the summit are cobbled with roundish rocks ranging from grapefruit to basketball size. It takes considerable commitment for a hunter to get up there at all.

But every season there was a gobbler or three on that flat summit. That's why, almost every year from 1985 until I moved away from the area in 2002, several spring mornings I sweated and strained and pulled my way to the top. More years than not, I eventually carried a gobbler back down.

There were only five days left in the '02 season when I climbed Heart Attack for the first time that spring, going in cold, guided only by faith. Faith can be a leaky vessel, but this time it was well-founded.

I started hearing two gobblers while I was still inching my way up the final hundred feet. But I was running late and was already behind the eight-ball. I'd misjudged the time it would take to make the climb, and they were already on the ground when I topped out. My breath was short and my pulse pounding, but no time for a breather now. I needed to close the distance and set up.

I said earlier that Heart Attack's summit was flat. It is, but that's misleading. "Flat" is a relative term in the Ouachitas. There was enough roll and fold up there for me to be able to get inside the 100-yard ring, and I sat to the gobblers – they'd gotten together immediately after flydown – with confidence. I got everything arranged and cast out my first call.

The results weren't exactly as desired. The birds had been gobbling every 20 to 30 seconds, but following my initial string of yelps they clammed up for a full ten minutes. When a nearby crow sounded off and they finally gobbled again, they'd moved 200 yards further away. I gave chase, but they'd lost their gobbling momentum and didn't make enough noise for me to keep track of them. On those infrequent occasions when they did gobble, each time they were farther away. The last time I heard them was at 10 a.m. – a sparkle gobble so faint I could barely make it out.

The next morning I allowed more climbing time. When gobbling time came I was red-faced and sweating, but on top. I was drawing in a deep breath to do some owling when a real barred owl saved me the trouble. The two gobblers answered him. I was less than 200 yards from both of them, and almost exactly in between.

It was a good place to be, so I settled in. They gobbled a lot on the roost, but since I couldn't hear any hens and the two gobblers had gotten together the day before, I figured they'd do it again. I stayed quiet and waited for things to unfold. It was hard to avoid feeling smug.

Hard, that is, until the gobblers flew down in opposite directions, leaving me in the center of a rapidly enlarging doughnut hole. By the time I realized they were both leaving, I was behind the eight-ball again. I never recovered. Ditto yesterday's hunt. I never heard a gobble after 10 a.m.

Day Three. Back on top, same listening spot, and both gobblers cranked up right on schedule. This time they were farther back on the plateau, and I crowded the harder-gobbling bird as much as I thought I could get away with. Maybe 75 yards. He flew down sort of toward me, but lit out of range, and the woods were too open for me to call to him while he was that close and in plain sight. He messed around for a half-hour within ten feet of his landing spot, strutting and gobbling, and then moved far enough north to drop out of view into a slight depression. I stroked out a run of soft yelps and he gobbled hard, walking on my last two or three notes.

I shouldered my gun and snicked the safety off. Twenty-five minutes later my arms were aching, and I lowered the gun. At twenty-five minutes and five seconds, he stepped out from behind a shortleaf pine tree at 15 yards, looking hard for the hen. Failing to spot her, he stepped back behind the tree. I got my gun back to my shoulder. I never saw or heard him again.

Day Four. Same story, different day. Both birds gobbled, and again they were a couple hundred yards apart. This time I picked the less-gobbling bird and was able to get within 50 yards of his tree. He sailed out at normal fly-down time, but evidently he and his buddy had patched things up, because they got back together and the day devolved into a repeat of the first – me following along behind two traveling gobblers who steadily increased their lead and quit gobbling at 10 o'clock.

I debated going elsewhere on the last day of the season, but it's hard to leave gobblers you've hunted four days in a row. The fifth morning started like all the rest, with two widely-spaced gobblers talking to each other on the roost. Again they got together on the ground. Again they led me around Heart Attack's flat crown. Again they shut up about 10 a.m.

But this day I didn't leave. Instead, I moved closer to where I'd heard the last gobbling, built a makeshift blind out of a few sticks and limbs, and took a nap. When I woke up, I made a series of lost calls, waited 30 minutes, then did it again.

I did this several times over the next few hours, and it was approaching 3 o'clock when I heard leaves crunching behind me. I scrooched into my hide as best I could and in a minute or two a black blob appeared in my right-side peripheral vision. Then it was two blobs.

The longbeards slowly worked their way farther into my field of view, and when they were past me I was able to get my gun slid around, keeping it low, until it was pointing the right direction.

Quick-drawing is almost always a recipe for disaster, but you don't have to quick-draw. When a gobbler is looking for a hen, you can often get away with a slow, smooth move to raise the gun. You won't have all day, but the gobbler is expecting movement and will usually come to attention long enough for you to get on him and pull the trigger.

That's what happened. They looked like twins standing there, and the one that didn't leave weighed 22 pounds. That's big for a Ouachita gobbler, and he had the kind of spurs that make turkey hunters smile.

I haven't been back to Heart Attack. I'll probably never go there again. I was 55 in 2002; you do the math. The mountain is no place for old men, and I know it. But if legs and lungs would still allow, I wouldn't hesitate to go in blind next spring.

There'll be a gobbler or two up there. I know that, too.

The Gobbler of Heart Attack Mountain

He had the kind of spurs that make turkey hunters smile.

28

The Surprise Gobbler

I read somewhere that a turkey's gobble contains 20-odd individual sounds. I don't know how accurate that is, but I do know this: When a gobbler is very, very close, you hear things in his gobble that are inaudible when he's farther away.

In this instance, I heard the deep, pulmonic rumble that provides the floor upon which the gobble itself is laid. I also heard the metallic rattle that starts toward the end of the gobble and continues a tenth of a second past the end of it. I also heard something I'd never heard before, but was unmistakable nonetheless: I heard his feathers rustle against one another as he settled back into normal posture following the gobble. It was a vaguely hissing sound and only lasted a second: *Fsssst.*

The gobbler that treated me to all these new sounds was directly behind me, no more than 10 yards away. Probably more like five. It was still dark and he was still in the tree.

Not dark enough, though, for me to risk trying to get a little farther from him. All I could do was lean against my tree and listen as he gobbled again several minutes later. Then he gobbled again, and again, and again. By the time the cardinals started singing, he was in full morning roar, sounding off every five to ten seconds and throwing in a double gobble every few minutes. I sat motionless as a roadkill, hoping he wouldn't hear me breathing or hear my heart pounding.

When he pitched out he flew directly over my head, 15 feet up. I could have shot him, but a lesson most turkey hunters learn early is that shooting at flying turkeys is a low-percentage play. His vital areas are usually hidden by the bulk of his body, and all you end up doing is filling his ass full of lead. Anyway, where would the enjoyment and challenge have been? So I sat tight and watched him sail off the bench, and after he was out of sight I stood up, stretched, and went to Plan B.

He started ground-gobbling almost as soon as he landed. He was less than 100 yards away under the lip of the bench, but it was steep down to his level and I didn't think he'd come back up. Another lesson turkey hunters learn early is that it's not easy to call a gobbler back to his roost tree.

So I backed off, walked 250 yards down my bench in a flanking move and, when I thought it was safe, dropped down to his level. He double-gobbled at my first call, and a few minutes later I saw him coming, far down through the open woods. He was still 150 yards away, strutting straight toward me and gobbling as he came, when a hen got into the mix. She strolled off the bench above the gobbler, walked in front of him like he didn't exist, and continued downhill off the second bench. He went behind a tree as he turned to follow her, and though he continued to gobble as he went downhill, I didn't see him again that morning.

It rained hard the next day and I surrendered to an attack of wimpiness and the siren call of my pillow. I took the day off and caught up on sleep. But the third day dawned clear and still, and I was there before first light. He was within 50 feet of where he'd been two days before, but this time there was more real estate between us. Since he'd flown to the lower bench that first day, I used the remaining dregs of the night to retreat, drop onto the bench below him, and close the distance until I was directly downhill and less than 75 yards away.

So naturally he decided this morning to just tilt forward and fall off his limb. I didn't hear him land, but when he gobbled on the ground it was a much more muffled sound because of the intervening lip of the bench. When I was sure he was down, I hit him pretty hard with an excited blend of cutts and yelps and he went crazy.

For a pretty good while it was tense doings. He'd approach the steep lip of the bench and I, 35 yards below, would get my gun aimed at the sound of his gobbling. Then he'd retreat from the edge and I'd relax a little. This went on for more than an hour, during which time he came almost to death's door a half-dozen times. Once I even caught a glimpse of his tail fan as he strutted at the edge of the bench. But he turned around a foot too soon, and the opportunity was lost.

I don't know what bumped him, but something did. I heard him putt several times, then heard heavy wingbeats, and suddenly the hunt was over. Coyote, maybe? Bobcat? Whatever, he was spooked and gone, and I heard him no more that morning.

I went back to him two times in the next four days. One day he gobbled three times, and the other day it was so windy I never heard him gobble at all.

Then I went to Missouri for a four-day hunt and got lucky, filling two tags in two days. I was scheduled to be in Kansas after the Missouri hunt, but the early tag-out left me with two down days. Turkey bums like me find that unacceptable, so I drove the 200 miles back home to give those two days to the bench-hopping gobbler.

The first morning was business as usual.

He did a lot of gobbling on the roost, and after flydown he worked in fairly close to my calling. But again he stayed out of sight, and eventually a hen led him off or he fell into a groundhog hole or Scotty beamed him up or something. All I know is he gobbled a lot at my calls for more than an hour, hung up on the bench below me, and stayed interested but invisible until he just quit gobbling about 9 o'clock. I stayed in there until 1 p.m. and never heard him again.

On the morning of the second bonus day, and my last chance to hunt him for the year, the gobbler flew down my way and approached until – again – he was just under the lip of the bench. I caught tantalizing glimpses of him for more than 50 yards as he slowly approached, but at

60 yards he dropped a little more downhill and I didn't see him again until the edge of that tail fan popped over the lip right in front of me at 25 yards. I had just enough time to swing my gun barrel 15 degrees to get on him before I saw the globe of his white noggin come up from behind the lip of the bench.

There's where he applied the brakes. I could see all of his head, but nothing below it, and after what seemed like ten minutes but couldn't have been more than three, he turned sideways and started easing back downhill.

Sideways is better than head on because it gives you a slightly bigger kill area. I tipped him over. He weighed 18 pounds, had a full, beautiful tail fan…and was a jake.

Surprise!

The Surprise Gobbler

Surprise!

29

The Multigobbler

He was a jake when we first met. My turkey log book pegs the date as April 24, 2016, and he came in dogging the steps of an eager-to-die three-year-old. The big gobbler answered my first call, then crossed a valley at forced-march speed. He paused behind a tree at 70 yards just long enough for me to get Ol' Betsy pointed in the right direction, then came walking at me in a comical quick-step that brought him from 70 yards to 25 yards in less than a minute. All the while, the acolyte jake zig-zagged along behind, shadow-gobbling, acting every bit the goofy, half-retarded adolescent we all know jakes to be.

When I pulled the trigger, the jake launched into a steep, climbing turn, changed his mind and fell out of his chandelle like Icarus. He started running away, but when the downed longbeard started flopping, the younger one came racing back, gobbling almost nonstop. He lost no time jumping on top of his boss, pecking, flogging and attempting to do damage with his nubby spurs.

I watched the show for a while and learned two things about his gobbling. First, he was remarkably full-voiced for an immature gobbler, and second, he was inordinately fond of double gobbling. Every other utterance, it seemed, was a double or triple gobble. After five minutes with no sign of a let-up, I shooed the jake away from my now-rumpled gobbler. He reluctantly left and walked over the slope into a nearby hollow, suspiciously eyeing me every step of the way. As far as I could hear him down through the spring woods, he gobbled.

Bad Birds 2

Double gobbled. Gobbled. Triple gobbled.

It's a sleeper location, on public land but close to a small community and right beside a busy state highway, and I had always held it in reserve. It's only a few miles from home, it rarely gets hunted and it always seems to hold a bird or two. So it came to pass that halfway through the 2017 Arkansas turkey season, after having my ass handed to me on numerous hunts, I went there blind.

There was only one bird gobbling, but almost every other utterance was a double or triple. *Hello turkey, my old friend. I've come to talk with you again.*

He was roosted within 100 yards of where I'd watched him flog his mentor almost exactly a year before, and I set up against the same tree I'd used then. Hey, why mess with a winner?

Every other gobble from this turkey, it seemed, was a double or triple.

The Multigobbler

After giving him a couple sleepy tree yelps to get him thinking my way, I shut up and let him gobble all he wanted to on the limb. He pitched down and I saw him do it; in my direction. As soon as he hit the ground he cranked up again. I yelped at him and he quickly closed the distance until he was just the other side of a little tater knob hill, close enough to kill as soon as he stuck his head up.

It's hard not to feel smug when you've got a hard-gobbling turkey in shotgun range. I didn't even try. A half-hour later, though, the edges of my grin were losing their curl. I hadn't called to him for 15 minutes. He was still racking off single, double and triple gobbles like he was suffering from an advanced case of turkey Tourette's, but he was still a no-show.

Then the volume and the direction of the gobbles abruptly changed, and in a minute or two I saw him walking through the woods 90 yards off the gun. He dropped into the head of the hollow he'd retreated to the year before, and as soon as he was out of sight I took off on a flanking maneuver to get ahead of him. He was too quick for me, though, and was going up the other side of the hollow before I got where I needed to be. We played follow-the-leader until a little after 10 that morning, when he got sore-throated or something and shut up.

It rained hard the next two days. I went out during lulls on both afternoons and tried to raise him, but all I succeeded in doing was getting soaked both times.

The next morning (April 24, coincidentally) dawned perfect: clear, still, cool. I figured he'd be talky, but nope. He gobbled twice on the roost (both singles) and twice on the ground (both doubles.) I stayed in there with him until noon, never heard him again, then left for Missouri.

Life went on, some turkeys died and others didn't, and it was 2018. I decided to hunt the Multigobbler on Opening Day this year. Jill and I had already had a good season, with kills in Hawaii, Texas and with our 11-year-old grandson during the Arkansas youth hunt.

But once again the Multigobbler wasn't buying what I was selling. He started gobbling across the hollow from where I'd worked him the year before, but I had time to get over there with him if I hurried. I made it, but I was feeling my age by the time I got there.

I've always been a counter; it's an annoying habit I can't shake. Thus I know he gobbled 217 times between first light and 6:45, when he finally left the limb and sailed all the way across the hollow I'd recently struggled through. He lit within 50 yards of the tater knob where I'd met him two years before and spent the next hour strutting and gobbling in place, while I hunkered helplessly just below the rim of the hollow. I couldn't get up on the flat with him because he was too close, and I couldn't call him to where I could see him because, much as I hate to admit it, I'm not good enough. It ended poorly: I tried a sneak, he saw me and left.

I hunted him twice more in 2018, made contact both times, and never to my knowledge got closer than 200 yards.

More life went on, more turkeys died and 2019 came. It was late in the season before I tried for the Multigobbler, and 30 minutes into gobbling time with no sound, I was beginning to believe he hadn't survived the intervening year.

I was wrong. I finally heard him – far, far away, almost too far to course – but I sorted it out and closed the distance as fast as I could. He'd abandoned his old haunts and was now roosted along a power line right-of-way right beside the busy state highway. He was nearly a mile from the tater knob and the hollow where I'd always hunted him. He was on the ground in the power line cut by the time I got there. His numerous double and triple gobbles left no doubt about his identity, and he still didn't want to play. After gobbling at me and every other sound for an hour or so, he walked east along the power line (I was west) and disappeared.

The next morning I was on the power line at first light, but he wasn't. No sirree. He was in the head of a hollow a half-mile north, on the other side of the most horrible cedar hell in the Ozark Mountains. I didn't think I could circle around it in time to get to him before fly-down, and you couldn't have driven me through the middle of that thing with a bullwhip. They don't call 'em cedar hells for nothing. So I went to Plan B, which involved leaving and hunting elsewhere. Dang me if it didn't produce a nice mid-morning gobbler on a mountaintop 15 miles away.

Flushed with success, I went back to the Multigobbler the next morning. Playing a hunch, I didn't go to the distant hollow beyond the cedar hell, but instead set up near where he'd roosted two days before. I hated the set-up; the highway was so close the lights of passing traffic lit me up like strobes through the trees. We're talking 75 yards here. Maybe less than that.

But I'd guessed right. When he started gobbling, he was as close as the highway, in a big shortleaf pine on the edge of the power line cut. There was a perfect landing zone in the cut 35 yards off my gun barrel. Once again, smugness set in. *Hello turkey, my old friend. I've come to talk to you again.*

So, what did the Multigobbler do? Well, after his usual serenade of singles, doubles and triples, he pitched out due south, sailed across the blacktop highway barely avoiding being hit by an 18-wheeler. He lit on the opposite road shoulder, gobbled once, then walked into the woods and shut up.

Now even more life has gone on, more turkeys have died, and in the fullness of time 2019 has become 2020. Turkey season isn't far off, and I've been thinking about the Multigobbler. Has he survived another winter? If so, he's a five-year-old, and his spurs will be something to behold. But he'll also be even harder to kill, because, well, you know. He's a five-year-old.

My best option, whether he's dead or alive, would probably be to forget about him. Life is short; turkey seasons are shorter yet. But I've already given him ten days of my life, and you know how it is when one gets under your skin.

What's another day or two?

Author's note: Hunted him twice during the 2020 season. Never heard a peep.

30

The Eddiceton Warrior

In my experience, every longbeard in Mississippi's Homochitto National Forest is a Bad Bird. I can show you the scars. But the one I called the Eddiceton Warrior was among the baddest. Not only did he whip turkey hunters, he also whipped his fellow turkeys.

We first crossed paths in 2009, when our Mississippi hunting buddy Andy Terrell showed Jill and me on a map how to get to a hard-to-reach chunk of "guvment" land he said had lots of turkeys. I'm as secretive as the next turkey hunter so I'll not get too specific here, but Andy's directions included passing through the small Franklin County community of Eddiceton and entering the national forest there. That's as close as I'll get you.

Andy was right about the turkeys. We'd spent two gobble-less days hunting other parts of the Homochitto, but our first morning at Eddiceton we heard 11 gobblers – a virtual wealth of turkeys for that part of the world, especially on public land.

As mentioned, though, every Homochitto bird is a Bad Bird, and even in that target-rich environment we were unable to make a sale that morning. Late that afternoon found us sitting on different ridges half a mile apart, trying to roost a bird.

It was after 6:30 and the shadows were long when I heard him gobble 300 yards up the creek bottom. At 7 he gobbled again, closer by half. Seconds later I saw him walking slowly through the bottom, headed my way. When he was 100 yards out, another bird gobbled behind him.

Bad Birds 2

Almost immediately I heard the fight start.

He swapped ends like somebody had popped him in the butt with a peashooter. Back up the bottom he went, purposeful, moving fast. He went out of sight, and almost immediately I heard the fight start. It was a quiet, windless afternoon and the ridges flanking the creek bottom funneled the sound well, so it sounded like the fight was right in my lap instead of 150 yards distant. But sound and fury was all I got that day. The fight ended, it got dark, I left after hearing no more gobbling.

Next morning we were listening from the ridge above where I'd last seen the gobbler. He sounded off on cue, 100 yards farther up the bottom and on the opposite ridge. It was too open in there for us to risk crossing the bottom to him, so we set up a couple hundred yards apart, one each side of his roost site. If he came up or down the bottom one of us might have a chance at him.

He came my way, but he was following three hens and everyone ignored my calling. The little group was almost out of sight when another turkey gobbled from the top of the opposite ridge. The one I was watching gobbled back, quickly and aggressively. He left his hens and started up the slope. The two gobblers met halfway, directly across from me at less than 100 yards, and this time I had a ringside seat.

The fight was violent but brief. The challenger wanted to strut and bluster, but never got the chance. The bird I'd been watching plowed into him like a bowling ball hitting a fresh rack of pins, and with much the same effect. The challenger found himself upside down in the leaves, getting his clock thoroughly cleaned. As soon as he could break away, he flopped/ran/flew out of there like his tail was on fire. The Eddiceton Warrior allowed him to go, gobbled once at the rapidly retreating form, and returned to his hens. I maintained contact with them for the next hour, and though he'd gobble at me, the hens kept pulling him steadily away. I gave up the chase when they crossed onto private land.

The third morning found Jill and me split up and listening from our respective second-day set-ups. The Eddiceton Warrior was home. He gobbled some, but again he wouldn't play. We did, however, hear him get into yet another fight – the third in three days – with a turkey that never gobbled. At least, we assumed it was a turkey. As cranky as the Warrior was, he might have been fighting a buzzard. Or a burned stump.

The only other turkey we heard that morning was nearly a mile away and across a well-traveled Forest Service road. After the Warrior left us, we retreated to the truck and drove around to that road, but another truck was parked there. Time for Plan C. It too failed, but I won't bore you with it.

Afternoon found me sitting against the same tree from which I'd first seen the Warrior. Again, he gobbled up the creek bottom soon after 6:30. Again, I saw him walking toward me at 150 yards. This time, no other gobbler interrupted his march toward what I figured would soon be the end of his pugnaciousness.

Because of the slope behind me, I was exposed but not silhouetted, and I knew as long as I sat still I'd be okay. But I still had to get my gun up, so I picked out a big pine tree between us and when he went behind it at a range of 50 yards I made my play.

Bad move. I misjudged the width of the tree, or the position of his head, or the speed of the rotation of the Earth, or something, because as the gun came to my shoulder everything went haywire. He didn't come out from behind the tree like I expected. Instead, he clucked four times, each cluck fainter as the Doppler Effect did its insidious work. When I saw him again he was 125 yards away and going back up the creek bottom, erect as a fence post, every survival instinct going full blast.

We rested him the next day and hunted an old familiar spot 30 miles north. Jill killed her half of what should have been a double while her husband shot overneath his half. Nuff said there.

Consequently, I was perched on a low limb the fourth and final morning we had available to hunt the Warrior, and the driving rain that greeted us at wake-up time didn't help my mood any. Jill was tired of this cagey old turkey and wanted to try a new spot she'd been eyeballing, so I dropped her off in the wet darkness and went back to Eddiceton alone.

I wasn't expecting much, but life is short and turkey seasons are shorter, you know? Nuff said there, too. I left my vest in the truck, donned a camo raincoat, and started the hunt with the bare minimum: shotgun, two extra shells, hat, headnet, gloves, shells and two diaphragm calls. Lo the Spartan turkey hunter.

I stopped to wait at the edge of the creek valley, feeling low and mean and sorry for myself. Daylight came slow, weak and soggy, and it was well after normal fly-down time when the Warrior gobbled so close it scared me. I was leaning against a big pine and he was in the pine next to it, the trees so close their limbs overlapped. When he gobbled again I picked him out, hunkered close to the trunk, wet as a mud turtle and looking as miserable as one of God's creatures can look.

But once he got started gobbling, he behaved like it was a clear, dry morning. I stood under him and watched. I thought about limb-swatting him and then making up a big lie to tell Jill and Andy and the rest of the world. Once I even raised my gun and put the bead on his neck. But I'd been a turkey hunter for 30 years without roost-shooting one, and as I write this that number is 40 and I can still truthfully make the claim.

So I waited and watched, knowing from past experience that turkeys usually don't sail off the roost when it was raining but more or less just fall to the ground very close to the roost tree. I hoped he'd do that this time and would land close enough for things to work out. My philosophy: if his feet are on the ground, he's fair game.

It was after 8:30 and still raining hard when he got tired of it and decided he might as well begin his day. I wasn't looking at him at that moment, but I heard his limb suddenly shed five gallons of

Bad Birds 2

water and heard two or three heavy wingbeats, and suddenly he was on the ground at 20 yards. He gobbled twice, then started walking away. When I made my move he saw it and increased his pace. I followed him with the barrel, but my glasses were so streaked and blotched with water I couldn't be sure I was on his head.

I never pulled the trigger, and it ended not with a bang but a splash. We went back to Eddiceton several times in 2010 and 2011, but we never heard another turkey fight.

The nice lady at the convenience store in Bude, Mississippi

Practically every gobbler in the Homochitto is a Bad Bird, but every once in a while things work out. Not with the Eddiceton Warrior, though.

31

The King of the Food Plots

About 7 miles south-by-southeast of our 30-acre postage stamp of land within the Ozark National Forest, a crow-foot ridge system launches from the summit of an unnamed mountain looming above Highway 5. The highway skirts the base of the east side of the mountain, and a rough Forest Service road winds its way along the edge of the north face. About halfway to the top, another even rougher road breaks off to the left and, behind a locked gate, climbs steeply and crookedly the rest of the way to the top.

That dumps you out at an old log yard at the juncture of the crow-foot ridge system that forms most of the mountain's south slope, and it's an excellent listening spot. You can hear a goodly portion of each of the three descending ridges from the yard, and each of those ridges has its own food plot. As the crow flies, the plots aren't 300 yards apart, but you know about those damn crows. They can fly.

Turkey hunters can't – not this one, anyway – and that's a shame in this instance, because between those three food plots are two of the roughest hollows in the county. They're deep, steep and rocky, and about every hundred yards or so you encounter a band of cedars as thick as a Labrador retriever's coat.

So now you know what I was up against.

As hard as that place was to reach, I'd never have known there was a turkey in it, for the simple reason that I'd never have climbed up there to check. But the gate barring the road had been open all winter fall and winter, and I'd driven it while trapping for bobcats and coyotes in January and February.

The place was absolutely lousy with turkey sign. Several times I saw hens up there while running my traps. The Forest Service locked the gate in early March to keep vehicles out, but I climbed up there two mornings just before turkey season and heard six gobblers one day and five the next. They were spread more or less evenly among the three ridges.

You can probably guess where I was on Opening Day. Sure enough, they gobbled – four of them this time. I went down the center ridge, partly because two of the birds were on it and partly because it had the gentlest terrain of the three.

When fly-down time came, three of the turkeys shut up, including the two on my ridge. Typical. The lone bird still talking was on the ridge to my east, toward the highway, and I knew from my hunting maps and visual observation from the highway that the slope from ridgeline to blacktop was steep as a ski jump. I didn't think he'd go that way.

So, when he started moving slowly up the ridge toward the listening spot, I hotfooted it along my ridge to cut him off. I beat him to the spot, but when I called to him he reversed gears and went back a hundred yards to the food plot on his ridge.

The terrain on the ridge was rough enough that I could get in pretty tight, but still he wouldn't do anything except gobble at me. Presently he fell off into the hollow that separated the ridge I was on from the one I'd just left, crossed it and went straight to the food plot where I'd been standing an hour earlier. By the time I got back around there to that middle plot, he'd disappeared.

I went elsewhere the next day, but the memory of all those gobblers pulled at me and I was back at the head of the crowfoot on the third morning. There were six gobblers this time, and three of them were on the center ridge. Down there I went again. Dummy up the gobblers did again, except for one. I wasn't sure if this was the one I'd tangled with earlier, but at least he was on the center ridge with me this time.

But not for long. He worked me a while, then fell off into the west hollow and went up on the westernmost ridge, the one I hadn't been to yet. I went back to the log yard, around the head of the hollow and got over there with him. This time he played but wouldn't commit. We danced around the third food plot for two hours, playing chess, and I saw him twice during that time. Once was at 80 yards when he went across the far corner of the food plot, and the second time was when he stuck his head around a shortleaf pine at 7 steps, straight off my left shoulder. We were equally surprised, and it didn't end well for me.

I rested him (and me) for two days, and in the interim killed a nice bird on private land in the other end of the county. I had three more days to hunt in Arkansas before leaving on turkey safari. I wanted this bird.

The first morning of the three, it rained like Noah's warm-up shower, but it didn't start until I'd already pulled the long climb to the log yard. They had just started gobbling (six of them) when the bottom fell out, and they all shut up. I stayed around up there until nearly 9 o'clock. The rain never slacked off, and I never heard another gobble. If I've ever been wetter on a turkey hunt I don't remember it.

The second morning was cloudy and threatening more rain, but I guess my wife is right: I'm a slow learner. So I went up there again. This time I got in an hour of fruitless hunting before another toad-strangler started, with five gobbling from the roost and the usual solo performer once they hit the ground and nobody at all coming to the gun. Again I descended the mountain wet as an oyster.

The third and final morning it was gorgeous and cool. Five gobblers talking again, but this morning two birds kept it up after flydown. Both were in the vicinity of the food plot on the middle ridge.

For once, I'd played it right. Instead of waiting to see where the

The King of the Food Plots was a legitimate limb-hanger.

talkative gobbler was, I'd rolled the dice and committed to the middle plot before ever hearing the first cardinal. When the gobbling started, I was at the north edge of the middle food plot, and the two gobblers were on either side of the ridge and just off the south end of the plot, 200 yards away.

They flew down within seconds of each other, into the south end of the food plot. I hit them with a sharp but short series of yelp-cutt noises almost as soon as their feet hit the ground, and they gobbled simultaneously and started moving my way.

When turkeys act right, killing them is easy. These two acted right. I never made another call as I watched them close the distance, strutting all the way. At 30 yards I clucked, and both heads came up.

I could have killed them both, but I didn't. They looked like twins, and both were good birds. I arbitrarily shot the one on the left and watched the survivor fly off the ridge in the direction of the highway.

32

Jay's Pet

If ever there was an easy-to-kill gobbler, it was this one. Every afternoon during the fall, winter and early spring, about an hour before fly-up time, he'd show up behind Jay's hay shed. I sat there a dozen afternoons over that time span, perched comfortably in the shadows among the round bales, watching him and lusting after his long hooks and heavy double beard.

Jay and I were feeding him, of course, along with the dozen or so does and two raghorn bucks that also came in most afternoons – rice bran for the deer, sunflower seeds for the gobbler. He'd pick up seeds for a while, and twice I saw him stick his beak into a hill of rice bran. Out of curiosity, I suppose. Toward sundown, he'd wander back through the pasture and enter the woods within 30 yards either side of a big open-grown hickory tree along Jay's south property line. He usually roosted in a cluster of overmature shortleaf pines on Jay's neighbor.

In exchange for turkey hunting privileges, Jill and I trap predators, beavers and otters on both Jay and his neighbor, so I'm pretty sure we had access to this gobbler across his entire home range. Enough of it to kill him, anyway, at the barn, at the hickory tree or at the shortleaf pines. We quit feeding both turkeys and deer a full month before turkey season, but habit is a powerful thing. Both years we hunted him, Jay's Pet kept coming to the barn until well after the spring season opened. We could have head-smacked him pretty much any afternoon we wanted to.

Jay's Pet would have been easy to kill, if you didn't care how you did it.

Jay's Pet

But "hunted" is the key word in that paragraph. We didn't want to assassinate this gobbler from a hay barn in the afternoon. We wanted to call him up in the morning and kill him fair and square, the way turkeys are supposed to be killed.

Jay's Pet, however, had different ideas. In the evenings he was predictable as a Holstein headed for the milking barn. In the mornings, not so much. No matter where we set up on this gobbler on the roost, he flew down a different way. We could call or not call, set up close or not so close, and none of it mattered. We even tried splitting up and setting up on either side of him, and he still got out of there without giving us a shot. That went on all the first season we hunted him, five or six days, I disremember which.

We worried about Jay's Pet all summer. Old gobblers do die, after all, and the close-up looks I'd gotten at his spurs left no doubt he was old. But come fall, when Jay and I started putting out sunflowers and rice bran, it didn't take him long to make an appearance. His double beard seemed a little fuller and longer, but I expect that was just wishful thinking. And those majestic hooks were unchanged. A true limb-hanger, that's what this old boy was.

His pattern of behavior was the same. He'd show up from a different direction each afternoon, but he would show up almost every day. He always left the same way, walking within shotgun range of the big hickory and roosting in the shortleaf pines.

He wasn't one of those 200-gobbles-before-flydown turkeys or anything like that, but on just about any spring morning you could expect him to gobble 30 or 40 times. That's plenty of noise to allow a hunter to make a reasonable set-up, and plenty of noise to make for an enjoyable hunt. But like the Chad Brock song says, "Thunder's just a noise, boys; lightnin' does the work." And never did the gobbler's thunder lead to a chance for either of us to launch the lightnin'.

Jill had found a turkey elsewhere she wanted to hunt, so on Opening Day we went our separate ways. I wanted another crack at

Jay's Pet. The first two mornings, he quietly circled behind me after gobbling a few times on the ground. The first day, he clucked sharply from very close behind me, and when I predictably flinched, I heard him running away.

The next morning he did it again, but this time I anticipated the move and adjusted my position. I saw him coming, but when he got close enough to kill he was behind a screen of thick stuff. With 1-1/2 ounces of TSS 9s at a range of 30 yards, I could have probably killed him through the brush, but "probably" isn't good enough with a worthy opponent like that. I held off, waiting for a clear shot.

It was not to be. He puttered around for a while behind the brush, strutting or not strutting as the mood struck him, gobbling every few minutes. But he never came into the clear and after a while he just wasn't there any more. You know how that stuff goes.

Jay's Pet wasn't the kind of bird you wanted to hunt every morning. As bad as I wanted to kill him, I didn't want to spend an entire season hunting what was starting to look like an impossible turkey. Anyway, we knew he'd always be there. Miss a day, miss a week, he'd still be there. Nobody else had hunting permission on either property, so we didn't have to worry about somebody else messing with him.

The other side of the coin was, he seemed determined not to die. Jill and I decided that if we actually wanted to hang a tag on an Arkansas gobbler, we needed to go hunt other Arkansas gobblers. That's what we did. Jill hadn't had any luck with the gobbler she'd been hunting and I didn't have any hot prospects at all, so we broke out the boat and went up on the lake. Wonder of wonders, in a few days we'd each killed a nice gobbler.

We had three more days to hunt at home before going out of state, and we vowed to devote all three of them to killing Jay's Pet. And that's what it took. The first two days were repeats of our past experiences, with him gobbling a decent amount before flying down and giving us the slip. The third and final morning he flew down our way and gobbled several times as he made his way slowly in our direction.

We'd discussed this possibility ahead of time, and when he went silent Jill wordlessly scooted around our tree to cover the back door. Five minutes later her shotgun released its lightnin', scaring her poor husband out of his wits. When I came back to earth, I leaned around the tree and raised an eyebrow.

She was already leaning out and looking at me. The grin on her face told it all.

He was every bit the bird we thought he was: 23 pounds (a steady diet of black oil sunflower seeds will do that,) 11- and 8-inch beards, and those curved hooks I'd been slobbering over for two years measured a gnat's eyelash shy of 1-3/8. I was very, very happy for my wife's good fortune.

The undeserving, ungrateful, self-centered…

He was every bit the bird we thought he was, and I was very happy for my wife's good fortune. S-u-u-u-ure I was.

33

The Iron Gobbler

I don't know, any more than you do, why turkey hunters get up morning after morning, venture forth into the pre-dawn, short of sleep and jangly from caffeine, alienating boss and family alike, all in a usually futile effort to kill what is essentially an overgrown chicken.

But we do it, year after year after year. This despite the fact that whatever it is that makes a turkey hunter a turkey hunter – whatever warp in the human psyche makes this aberration possible – there are always gobblers out there that make us question just why in the hell we do it.

The overgrown chicken I came to call "The Iron Gobbler" was one of those birds. He lived on a beautiful cattle-hay-corn-wheat farm in east-central Kansas. The property was divided by three small creeks that prevented the horizon-to-horizon crop fields and pastures that are the norm farther west in the state. All three creeks were bordered by decently wide belts of good riparian habitat: big roost trees, shady, cool corridors to shelter and hide turkeys, permanent water. In short, it was as nice a place for turkey hunting as you could have wanted.

We hunted there, Jill and I, for a half-dozen years during the first decade of the century. It was a sweet honey hole, a bird nest on the ground, and (assuming we avoided making too many boneheaded mistakes) we could be confident we'd kill a couple gobblers there every spring.

This particular spring, during what I think was our fourth year of hunting the property, we'd already killed one of them. It was a husky if nubby-spurred two-year-old, and Jill subtracted it from a gang of six classmates that frequented the north end of the property. The next morning she went back for another one while I decided to try for a bird we'd heard on the south end. He'd gobbled a lot while Jill was killing her bird, and there didn't seem to be any other gobblers down there with him. No vocal ones, anyway.

There were two open areas on the south end of the property, separated by one of the creeks. One was a winter-grazed hayfield, the other a stand of winter wheat that was just breaking dormancy and beginning its spring growth spurt. I was waiting for daylight on the east side of the creek (the wheat field side,) but when things started happening and the gobbler flew down, it was into the hayfield on the west side. Of course.

I crossed the knee-deep creek in my ankle-deep boots and eased to the edge of the cover, setting up at a big sycamore at the barbed wire fence that kept the cows out of the wheat. He was strutting 80 yards into the greenery, no hens in sight, and I had no trouble coaxing him inside the 40-yard circle.

It was looking like one of those easy hunts that come along once or twice a year. You know the ones I'm talking about. The ones that give you the false hope that you've finally got this stuff figured out. Anyway, from the first sighting to the time I had him killable was less than five minutes, and I was milking the moment, not quite ready for it to end.

He had his left side to me, tucked deep into his strut, and I was looking down the barrel and waiting for him to raise his head when Jill's shotgun roared a half-mile north. It startled both the gobbler and me. He periscoped. I rushed the shot.

He went down, but didn't stay there. Executing a snazzy gymnast's shoulder roll, he regained his feet and ran like a cheetah, quicker than I can tell you about it.

I normally hold off shooting at running turkeys, but this one was already hit and I made an exception. I swung ahead of him, the way you'd lead a running rabbit, and sent another 2 ounces of 5s his way. He hit the ground a second time, but again he got up as fast as he fell and this time he got airborne. He was struggling, but he was flying.

I normally don't shoot at flying turkeys, either, but this one was hard-hit, not once but twice. I racked the 870 and launched another round. It was wasted shot and powder, though. Rattled as I was by then, I'm pretty sure that third try was a clean miss. I staggered to my feet and watched him sail into the tree line at the end of the field.

I'd already been looking for him for more than 30 minutes when Jill showed up, carrying another two-year-old. She'd heard all the racket and come to the obvious conclusion: one shot, good news; two shots, well, maybe; three shots, uh-oh! When she heard my barrage, she shouldered her gobbler and came to help me find mine.

After a brief explanation of what had happened, we walked to the end of the wheat and resumed the search. I'd pulled the trigger at 6:55, and we stopped looking at noon.

If you've ever seriously wounded a gobbler and failed to recover it, you know exactly how I felt. We'd already taken our allotted two birds from that farm – actually three, or so we thought at the time – so we hunted elsewhere for the rest of our time in Kansas that year.

The following spring, there were more gobblers on the property than we could keep track of. Once again, though, they were concentrated on the north half of the place, with at least a dozen birds roost-gobbling up there. Only two birds were gobbling on the south end.

As before, Jill went north and I took the much quieter south end. As before, I was watching my two gobblers strut in the same field where I'd crippled the longbeard a year ago. As before, Jill's shot from up north startled both me and the gobblers I was watching. The difference was, this time I wasn't looking down my gun barrel when my wife pulled the trigger. I remember thinking, *This is getting monotonous.*

Her shot brought both gobblers out of strut. They stood still as yard ornaments, looking for danger, and before they calmed down they took a few nervous steps in various directions. The bigger of the two walked with an obvious limp. It got me wondering.

The gobblers had been answering my calls for an hour, but neither had come closer than about 80 yards. I always carry one of those folding silk-screened strutting gobblers in my vest, and though I don't often use it, I figured this was the time to give it a try. I found a dead branch to use as a stake, belly-crawled to the edge of the field and stuck the thing in the ground. By the time I'd wiggled back to my tree, both gobblers were eyeballing the decoy.

They were cautious, though, and for a long time it appeared it wasn't going to work. But finally they started edging gradually closer. I kept my eye on the gimpy one, and when he raised his head at 35 yards I took him down.

It was a replay of the previous year's nightmare. I blew half a pillow's worth of feathers out of his breast, and unbelievably, he was up again and running, with no hint of a limp. He was 60 yards out before I recovered, so I didn't shoot again. I watched him disappear into the brush at the south end of the field within ten yards of where the crippled gobbler had gone in the year before, and after gathering my wits and cussing and kicking things and stomping on my hat, I went down there and started looking. Jill joined me, having again killed a north-end gobbler.

Long story short, we searched for four hours without finding a feather. Before we left the farm, I hung a feed sack on a fence and shot it from 30 yards. My EOTech sight was way off, sending the payload more than a foot below point of aim. As I'd suspected from all the feathers, I'd body-shot the turkey.

Again it was a sickening feeling, but at least this time I knew what had caused it. I took the sight off the gun that afternoon, and the next morning found us on the south end of the property. This time we were hunting together.

We put out two hen decoys in front of the silk-screened gobbler and were comfortably set up on the edge of the field when the gobbling started. We could hear the big wad of turkeys on the north end of the property, and Jill was second-guessing her decision to hunt the south end with me. But we did, after all, have two birds gobbling close by. They flew down into the field and immediately spotted our little spread. Both turkeys gobbled aggressively and lost no time heading our way.

They came in on Jill's side, coming from left to right. When the first gobbler was easily killable I clucked sharply with a diaphragm. He stopped and straightened up. She killed him with a clean, devastating jellyhead shot at less than 20 yards. The second bird immediately took flight, and, though I badly wanted to, I obeyed my personal taboo and didn't shoot at him.

Jill's gobbler had a broken and healed left shank (the scaly, hairless part of the leg,) which explained the limp. When we dressed him later that morning, other things were explained. We found several old, healed shot scars in the left side of his breast, along with a half-dozen fresh, bloody ones. His left breast was horrible-looking – bloodshot, bruised yellow-and-green. We threw it away.

The evidence was convincing. The healed shot wounds and the broken shank were from my unsuccessful attempt to kill him a year before. The fresh wounds were from my too-low shot the day before. All those wounds, old and new, were on the gobbler's left side – the side that had been toward me on both my attempts – but the side away from Jill when she'd killed him.

He'd taken three solid hits in two years, one of them less than 24 hours before, and still came in strutting to whip an interloper. Talk about tough.

Iron Gobbler indeed.

After getting shot all to hell by the author, The Iron Gobbler died easily under the gun of the author's wife Jill Easton.

Lagniappe

*According to the Oxford Dictionary,
lagniappe is "something given as a bonus or extra gift."
Here ya go. You're welcome.*

34

In It to Win It

If a game is worth playing, it's worth playing to the best of your ability. Otherwise, you might as well stay home.

"Man, I wish I was as good at turkey hunting as you are," the guy said as I was autographing his copies of *Bad Birds* and *Turkey Hunting Digest*. "I'd love to be able to kill as many gobblers every spring as you do."

He looked to be in his late 20s, maybe 30, and he had the same fire in his eyes that used to burn in my own. We were in Nashville, both of us drawn to the annual NWTF convention like moths to a flame. I handed him the books, and he accepted them like Moses taking the tablets. I shrugged my shoulders and grinned at him.

"How many days did you hunt last spring?" I asked. He told me he'd hunted four mornings and had tagged one bird.

"Well," I said, "you need to rethink this. I took seven birds last spring, but it took me 46 days of hunting to do it. If you want to use total poundage as your measure of success, then yeah, I guess I beat you. But if you score it by hunting days per bird taken, you're doing quite a bit better than me."

It was a prime example of the universal truth that all things are relative. The young man stood there and thought about it for a second, then shook my hand. He walked away with his shoulders back and his chest puffed out just a little, feeling much better about his single-bird

Bad Birds 2

You might pick up a tip or two from a book like the one you're holding or the one shown here, but don't count on it. Experience is the best teacher.

tally for the previous spring.

What I didn't tell that guy, though, is that I probably *was* a better turkey hunter than he was when we had that conversation ten years ago. And it's not because I was born with an overdeveloped Leatherstocking gene or anything like that; I know a whole bunch of turkey hunters who are far, far better at this game than me, and no season goes by without more than one gobbler leaving me feeling like the village idiot. But experience truly is the best teacher, and I'd spent much more time on the hunt than that young man. That one spring alone, I hunted nearly 12 days to his one. When you spend that much time doing something, you start to figure a few things out. Things rub off on you, and lessons learned in the School of Hard Knocks tend to stick.

To put it another way: If you haven't learned a few tricks of the trade after that much practice, it's probably time to start thinking about changing hobbies.

For some of us, however, calling turkey hunting a "hobby" is like saying a pigeon-grade Parker is a double-barreled shotgun. It's a true statement, as far as it goes, but it stops way, way short of the whole story. Turkey hunting, to people like me, is so much more than that. It's a way of life. It's the pillar around which we hard-cores build our entire year.

I fell into the abyss on a gorgeous late-March morning in 1976, when a friend took me on my first turkey hunt near Natchez, Mississippi. I had been a hunter since the age of six or seven, but turkeys were scarce as tyrannosaurs in my part of the world, Therefore, I never got exposed when I was young. But in that spring of my 30th year, everything changed. Standing on a ridge in the Tunica Hills, as the light began to grow, I heard not only my first wild turkey gobbler, but also my second, third, fourth, fifth, sixth and seventh, all in the space of about ten seconds, each one of them eager to out-shout the others.

There's only one way to describe the result of that experience: it ruined me. Until then, I'd considered myself fairly well adjusted. But after hearing that eruption of gobbling all around me, I became an instant turkey junkie.

I didn't kill a bird that morning. Nor did I kill one that spring. Nor, for that matter, the next year, or the year after that. Or the year after that. I was the greenest of greenhorns. I had nobody to show me the ropes, and how-to turkey hunting information was as hard to find back then as honest politicians are today.

Here's how ignorant I was: I didn't even know how to position a diaphragm call in my mouth. On my first solo hunt, I stuck the thing in vertically, reeds touching my tongue and the back of the horseshoe against the roof of my mouth. The pathetic sounds I was able to coax out of the call in that position sounded just about like you'd expect – which is to say, hideous.

When you're that innocent of knowledge, when you're so inept you don't even recognize your mistakes as mistakes, you are pretty much guaranteed to fail. And fail I did, in epic fashion.

During those early years, I made every blunder you can imagine, and a few I'm pretty sure you can't. I got too close to birds on the roost. I set up too far away from others. I blew birds away from me by calling too much. I let others get bored and walk off because I called too little. I called a few birds into gun range or nearly so, but managed to flub it every time by moving too soon or too late, or letting them pick me out, or hiding so well I couldn't see the gobbler to kill it when it got there. If there was a way to screw up a turkey hunt, I discovered it and employed it during those five dismal, frustrating springs.

About the only thing I did right was keep trying. I stayed after them, hunting at every opportunity and as long as possible into the day – from sunrise to sunset, if I could manage it. Even being as green as I was, I knew if I was going to ever succeed, I had to build time in the woods. I had to figure things out, I had to learn from my mistakes,

In It to Win It

Jason Hart, a partner in Nomad and Huk outdoor clothing, is most definitely an "in it to win it" guy.

I had to capitalize on my infrequent opportunities to shoot turkeys.

It took the intervention of a more experienced hunter to help me set that first one to flopping. Robert read of my troubles in a weekly outdoor column I was writing at the time for the local small-town daily, and he took pity on me. He took me hunting on two consecutive Saturdays in late April. The first hunt was uneventful; we hunted from can see to can't see without hearing a gobble or seeing a feather.

But midway through the morning on the second Saturday, we located an inexperienced two-year-old gobbler. Robert called it in and I shot it. I remember standing over that scrawny, pencil-bearded gobbler, shaking Robert's hand in the late April sunlight, listening to him say "Okay, buddy, now you're on your own." Except, of course, he didn't say buddy.

I also remember thinking: *Dammit! Now I've really gotta learn how to do this.*

And slowly, oh so slowly, I did figure it out. More or less. It took a while, and there were precious few brilliant flashes of light in the process, but the *aha!* moments began to accumulate as the hunting days piled up. And a few beards began to show up in the mothballed cigar box beside the dinky beard of that first suicidal two-year-old. Eventually, with many false starts and backslides along the way, I developed into a fairly decent turkey hunter. Or at least I am whenever I can find a gobbler that's willing to play.

Full disclosure: I've had a few big advantages in my haphazard journey up this learning curve. When you write about turkey hunting for national magazines, you sometimes get invited on hunts with high-profile turkey hunters. So it came to pass in my early years as a turkey chaser that I got to participate in hunts with such luminaries as Brad Harris, Eddie Salter, Michael Waddell, Harold Knight, Ray Eye, Bill Jordan, Toxey Haas, Bo Pittman, Ron Jolly, Larry Norton, Ricky Joe Bishop, David Blanton, Bob Walker, Gary Sefton, Steve Stoltz, Cuz Strickland and others. But even though all these guys taught me a lot

In It to Win It

Even the best get beat. Ray Eye, here autographing copies of his excellent book, Ray Eye's Turkey Hunter's Bible, *would be the first to tell you that.*

of the tricks and techniques I use today, perhaps the most valuable thing these accomplished hunters collectively taught me is that no one – *no one* – is immune from getting his nose rubbed in it. I've watched every one of the above-mentioned hunters get beat by wary gobblers.

Without exception, these skilled veterans have handled their defeats with aplomb and grace. And I learned that from them, too. Yeah, sure, I've seen a few hats thrown to the ground and stomped on when a particularly aggravating bird does the dirty deed and gets away. But hey, who among us hasn't stomped a hat now and then?

On the baseball field, such behavior is unsportsmanlike and will earn you an early shower, but in the turkey woods it's an acceptable way to blow off steam after yet another drubbing by a turkey gobbler. That is, it's acceptable as long as you get over your snit, pick up your hat, straighten the bill and get on with the hunt.

And to repeat what was said a couple paragraphs back: it was valuable to learn the "experts" also routinely get their butts handed to them. Maybe not quite as often as we peons down here in the real world, miles beneath the rarefied air occupied by the sure-nuff turkey hunters of the world, but at least the heavy hitters get beat often enough to make me feel better about myself and my marginal talents.

You probably think having this kind of first-hand knowledge about the track record of the experts would be pretty useless. You're wrong.

Knowing the big boys also get their noses rubbed in it allows me to summon the mental strength, resolve, or whatchawannacallit that helps me keep on plugging away, day after day, week after week, season after season. On every hunt, I do the best I can under the circumstances of the moment. When I'm successful, I enjoy the glow and do the requisite amount of slapping my own back, but I take no illusions of grandeur from it. When I lose, which is most of the time, I take my lumps and move on. My friend Tom Kelly once wrote me in a letter more than 25 years ago: "I just get in there and swing the bat, and whatever happens, happens."

That's the key. Keep swinging the bat. No matter what you're talking about – golf, fly fishing, Texas hold 'em, badminton – if you want to become better than just so-so at it, you have to do more than simply *love* it. You have to get out there and *do* it. As frequently as possible.

Because the world is a busy and complicated place, it's an investment most hunters are not willing (or able) to make. Other things tug at us, competing for time, attention and money. Family responsibilities, job duties, the ubiquitous World Wide Web, "smart" gadgetry, video games, a myriad of other recreational choices, job duties, all chip away at our time. And no one has been able to figure out how to cram more than 24 hours into a day.

All of which is beside the point. Every bit of it. If you want to pull yourself out of the mediocrity that grips most turkey hunters like the LaBrea Tar Pits gripped dinosaurs, you *must* make the commitment to spend as much time in the actual pursuit of turkeys as you can. Not thinking about it, understand, but doing it. Watching videos and attending conventions and seminars, reading magazines and books – like, for instance, the one you're now holding – are important, make no mistake about it. But it's hands-on experience, and that alone, that will take you to the next level as a turkey hunter.

Every old hippie and stoner from the 1960 and '70s is familiar with the English rock group Dire Straits. In one of their trademark songs, called "News," there's this lyric: *"It may be a game, but I won't play to lose."* In other words: "I'm in it to win it."

That's the prerequisite attitude for a good turkey hunter. No matter how good you get, you'll still lose more than you win. But never leave the truck thinking that losing will be the day's outcome. The odds say that, but never, ever think it.

Not to put too fine a point on it, but you only get one ticket on this merry-go-round called life. I decided long ago that, before my race is run, I was going to make myself into the best turkey hunter I can possibly be.

I'm not there yet, but I'm gaining on it. Oh, so slowly, I'm gaining.

35

All You Have to do is Try

Learning the ropes is hard – but not impossible

"**I do not** *hunt turkeys because I want to, I hunt them because I have to. I would really rather not do it, but I am helpless in the grip of my compulsion.*"

That was Tom Kelly in 1973, in his iconic book *Tenth Legion*. Kelly is a veteran of both WWII and the Korean unpleasantness, and was a bird Colonel of the Artillery Division when he retired from the armed forces somewhere around 1980. Beyond that, though, the Colonel was, still is as of this writing, a hunter, a deeply cerebral one. In that classic piece of literature, he brought forth the idea that turkey hunters are members of a subculture, and as a subculture he likened them – us – to Rome's durable, tough, invincible Tenth Legion.

In the 33 words that began this chapter, Colonel Kelly summed up the complex mix of passion, wonder, desire, helplessness, hope, need, frustration, joy, anger, disappointment, gratification – and yes, compulsion – that combine to make up this complex, multi-faceted thing we call turkey hunting. (If you've never read *Tenth Legion*, shame on you. Correct this oversight immediately by going to tomkellyinc. net and ordering a copy. You can thank me later. I like Maker's Mark, Blanton's and Jim Beam Black.)

Like most subcultures, this is a cult easily joined. But it's not quite so easy to fully fit in. Turkey hunting has its unique ins and outs, its own language and catch-phrases, its specific details, lore and sidelines. For the newcomer, it can be pretty overwhelming.

Much of this peripheral stuff, though, is easy enough. You can learn a lot of it without even going on a hunt.

Calling, for example. What with all the hunting shows on satellite TV, plus DVDs, seminars, calling contests, YouTube videos and other online resources, anyone with an average amount of dexterity, an ear not made of tin and a little time to practice can quickly learn to make the basic sounds required to call in a turkey.

Likewise, the theory of turkey hunting is fairly straightforward. It's the process by which a hunter uses skill, experience, gamesmanship, patience – and, usually, a generous dollop of luck – to bring a gobbler within 40 yards and then kill it.

Simple, right? Well, as anyone who's tried it knows, saying all those things is a hell of a lot easier than doing them. This is the very thing that makes turkey hunting addictive, but it's also what keeps so many beginners from actually becoming accomplished turkey hunters. They watch these 30-minute hunting shows, and they see turkey after turkey march in and die. The whole hunt lasts four minutes. Common sense tells us these hunts are necessarily shortened so they'll fit the time slot and so they won't bore the viewer to tears, but still the flash-bang speed of the action leads to subliminal, unreasonable expectations when the beginner actually goes hunting.

The previous chapter explains this next in detail, but here's the nut: Based on the hunting shows he's seen on TV, the beginner expects turkey hunts to unfold at a dizzying pace, with the turkey coming to the gun and presenting himself to be killed within a minute or two after the first call of the hunt. In the real world, the Cubs win the World Series about as often as this happens. Even if a gobbler does come fast, getting it to come that last few yards and then present itself for a killing shot doesn't always happen. Too many things can go horribly wrong all along the way, and these things are rarely shown or even mentioned on TV.

This sets the stage for massive disappointment. The typical

All You Have to do is Try

beginner goes out two or three times, gets thoroughly whipped, and quits in disgust. I was more stubborn than most; it took me four years to finally get discouraged and quit. When a gobbler walked up 10 feet behind me one April morning in that fourth year, putted and blew out of my life forever, I got up, stomped my hat into the mud, and vowed to never hunt turkeys again. I meant it.

But a friend heard about it and refused to let me quit. The story has been told in some detail in a previous chapter, so no need to rehash it here. Reader's Digest version: Robert called a longbeard up in my face, and despite the worst case of the yips I've ever experienced, I managed to kill it.

That bird was a late-hatched two-year-old, maybe 16 pounds, with candy-corn spurs and a skinny beard the size of a carpenter's pencil, but to me it was a trophy beyond measure. Still is, for that matter; it was my first one, you see. More importantly, it proved to me firsthand that yes, it could be done.

Gaining confidence, that's the key. With persistence and luck, you can get there on your own, but the road is full of potholes. During those four years I was flying solo, I crashed through turkey hunts like a wrecking ball through a balsawood barn. I made mistakes I didn't even recognize as mistakes, then doubled down on them. I moved on turkeys when I shouldn't have. I didn't move on turkeys when I should have. I'd get too close to a roosted bird, bump him, then get timid and set up way, way too far from the next one. I didn't know how to use terrain to my advantage, and therefore set up in inappropriate places. About the only mistake I didn't make was riding a horse through the woods and trying to catch a turkey in a landing net.

My early turkey hunting years would have gone much better if I'd sought the counsel of a friend like Robert when the bug first bit me, instead of wasting four springs trying to learn it on my own. It was only through luck that Robert heard about my decision to quit, and I was even luckier when he decided to help me out of the abyss. (Or into

Having the right relatives can help you gain both confidence and knowledge. Emma Van Dorn's grandfather is Brad Harris, and the author knows firsthand you couldn't ask for a better turkey hunting mentor. This is Emma with a six-bearded Missouri gobbler. Yes, you're reading that right.

it, depending on your point of view.)

The thing is, back then it was hard to find a turkey hunter willing to help. Turkeys were already well on the road to the astonishing recovery we're enjoying today, but hunters were just becoming aware of this "new" opportunity. There wasn't much information available to help them get better. Further complicating things was the fact that most of this new breed of hunters who were beginning to piece things together were close-mouthed about what they'd learned.

Things are vastly different now. Today's beginner doesn't have to go it alone. It's not hard to find a mentor, someone who will, if properly approached, help a beginner get started right. Internet forums like Gobbler Nation (www.gobblernation.com) are a good bet, but so are the circle of friends most of us already have. Chances are, you already know someone who can help.

Turkey hunting is not an idle hobby, and it's vital that the beginner realizer that fact from the get-go. It is, as has been previously mentioned, a cult. Turkey hunting is expensive, frustrating, addictive and time-consuming. It has resulted in divorces, bankruptcies, lost promotions and firings. Thank goodness, that's not the norm; most of us, no matter how fanatical, manage to keep our wives, jobs and credit rating.

Turkey hunting is to all other forms of hunting as prime rib is to hamburger. It is the supreme challenge. You are going up against an animal whose sense of awareness and acuity of hearing and eyesight are beyond compare. Calling a mature gobbler in and killing it fair and square is the pinnacle. Ask any veteran turkey chaser. Like Tom Kelly.

Here's some more Kelly wisdom to wind this down, this from the last page of *Tenth Legion:*

"*The first turkey that ever came to me on the ground did it a long time ago. I sat there with my hands shaking and my breath short and my heart hammering so hard I could not understand why he could not hear it. The last turkey that came to me last spring had exactly the same effect, and the day that this does not happen to me is the day that I quit."*

You can't sum it up any better than that. If you want that kind of adrenaline rush, become a turkey hunter. Here's Colonel Kelly again: *"Let me deliver the only final and absolute rule that must be followed to achieve membership in the Legion. All in the hell you have to do is try."*

There are plenty of us out here willing to help you. All you have to do is try.

All You Have to do is Try

All you have to do is try…

36

The Loaner Gun

The ongoing story of a traveling shotgun

April 23, 1993: hot, clear, muggy. It's my first Rio Grande turkey hunt, and I'm doing it in style, as a guest of Realtree on a 40,000-acre ranch near Alice, Texas. I'm 46 at the time. I've been chasing turkeys – always Easterns until now – for nearly 20 years, and I'm beginning to think I've learned a few things. Subsequent years will prove me wrong, but those are other stories.

Bill Jordan, Realtree founder and host of the hunt, has sent me into a 2,000-acre section that, as it turns out, is stiff with uneducated, unsophisticated gobblers. In the first 90 minutes I've called seven longbeards into range. So far I've let them all walk; hunts like this are beyond my ken, and I'm in no hurry to make it end.

After Longbeard Number 7 walks away unharmed, I move toward a bird I've been hearing for a while now. He's not far away, but there's a dense mesquite hell between us and I'm not eager to fight my way through it. But I can get within 100 yards of him without entering the thick stuff, and after I've done that I hit him hard with a box call. He cuts my yelps with an equally hard double gobble. Thirty seconds later he gobbles again, much closer this time.

I am set up and ready, and a good thing, too, because mere seconds later I see his feet approaching rapidly along a deer trail through the thicket. I have barely enough time to shift my gun barrel when he steps into the open at 15 yards and comes to an erect, searching stop. He looks five feet tall as I watch him over the gun.

The gobbler is in full sunlight, I am in deep shadow. Nothing separates us but air. He is mine any time I want him, but as mentioned, I'm in no hurry. I look him over, snood to toenails. His head and neck display the fiery red and almost startling white all turkey hunters long to see, his bluish caruncles all but swallowed by the surrounding white. The flat place below each eye is a strange but beautiful amalgam of iridescent red and maroon I've never seen before on a gobbler. His beard is thick, full, odd-looking; I suspect a double though I can't say for sure. His breast feathers are dark as a cave, but they cast a metallic sheen like oil on still water. His spurs make me gasp; at 15 yards, in full sunlight, they stand out against the white dirt path like tapered ice picks.

He is, in short, magnificent.

It flashes through my brain that he is almost too fine a bird to kill, but the silly thought leaves as quickly as it came. Pass this one up? Fat chance. There is no denying Longbeard Number 8.

I must have snickered or snorted or emitted some other dismissive sound when I was having that ridiculous catch-and-release thought, because just then the gobbler did the trademark wing-shuffle that signals a soon-to-depart turkey. He turned and took the first step back along the deer trail that would take him quickly out of sight. I didn't let him take the second.

My double-beard suspicion had been wrong. He had three. Back at camp, he weighed 22 pounds, impressive for a south Texas Rio. His beards measured 10-1/2, 8-1/2 and 6-1/2 inches, and his spurs were twin 1-3/8-inch daggers.

This was before Realtree's current association with Remington, and the shotgun du jour was a Mossberg 835, the first commercially available shotgun chambered for 3-1/2-inch loads. The Realtree folks had several 835s on loan that spring, all in original Realtree camo. The next day I killed a second good longbeard with that gun, this one at more than three times the range of the first, and I fell in love with that ugly, stubby, mule-kicking, turkey-stomping 835.

At the end of the hunt I asked Bill if I could buy the gun. He said no, not right then, but I could buy it after turkey season was over. But Bill lied. I reminded him about it after the season ended, and instead of selling it to me, he sent it to me as a gift. For more than a decade thereafter, it was my turkey gun. It was a good one, too – dependable, rugged, tight-shooting and devastating on 40-yard gobblers.

Fast forward a quarter-century. As much as I loved it, the old 835 was heavy as a concrete block and kicked like a howitzer. As I got older and less fond of unnecessary punishment, I laid it down in favor of other shot launchers that were more portable and didn't rattle my teeth every time I pulled the trigger.

It was a week before the 2018 turkey season. I was standing in the seldom-travelled gravel road in front of my rural home, guardedly comparing scouting notes with my neighbor Patrick and his 15-year-old son Clayton. I asked Clayton what gun he hunted turkeys with.

"This year I'll be using my trap gun," said Clayton, who competed on his high school shooting team. "It's an H&R trap model. It's got too much barrel, though. I'm saving up to buy a Mossberg 835. I won't have it this season, but next year I will."

"Hold on a minute," I said, and went into the house. Returning with the well-used Bill Jordan 835 and a box of 3-1/2-inch turkey loads, I handed both to the teenager. "Why don't you shoot this one this spring? Make sure it's really what you want."

I told Clayton how I'd come to be in possession of the gun, and his eyes widened when I mentioned Bill Jordan's name. The camo titan was one of his heroes. The boy held the battered old cannon in both hands, staring at it like it was a precious artifact. Which, of course, it was.

After the 2018 season ended, Clayton and Patrick brought

Clayton Thompson with a fine gobbler taken with the old Mossberg 835.

the 835 back, along with seven shells from the 10-pack box. Clayton had wisely burned one shell at a paper target, to check both pattern and point of impact and to get the feel of the gun. With the other two missing shells, he'd killed two fine gobblers. Both were at 40-plus yards, and both were clean, dead-right-there kills.

"I sure appreciate you loaning me this," he said, reluctantly handing me the 835. "I'm absolutely sure I want one now."

"Well," I said, "let me ask you a hypothetical question. If someone was to give you a gun like this, like Bill Jordan did me, do you think you could hunt with it for a few years and then pass it on to somebody else who was young and just getting started in turkey hunting?"

"Well, yeah," Clayton said, a little puzzled. "I guess I could."

I handed the Mossberg back. "Then this gun is yours for now. You don't have to do it anytime soon, but I'm putting you on your honor here. You have to promise me you'll give it to some other young hunter you think is worthy and who'll agree to pass it on to someone else when the right time comes."

There are moments you remember. We all have them, clear as crystal, on instant recall. One of mine, now, is the expression on that young man's face as he looked first at the gun, then at his dad, then at me. I don't remember what he said next, but I'll not forget that look.

Not long after, I was telling the story to my old friend David Blanton, Bill Jordan's right-hand man at Realtree.

"I love it!" David said. "What's Clayton's address? I'll get Bill to write him a letter about the gun and how he came to give it to you."

And Bill did, even though he got the date wrong by a few years. So now my young friend Clayton not only has a fine turkey buster in his custody, but also a letter of provenance, on Realtree stationery, to support it.

He also bears a solemn and important responsibility. Granted, it's only important to a tiny universe: himself, Bill Jordan, David

Blanton and me. But it's no less important because of its narrow scope. As Bill said in his letter: "It's nice to know that after Jim and I are both long gone, that old gun is still going to be killing turkeys, and that we were both links in the chain of its history."

Enjoy your shotgun, Clayton. Use it well and long. But be sure, be very damn sure, that someday you honor your covenant and pay that pump gun forward.

We need to keep this thing going.

The former and current custodians of The Loaner Gun, with one of its more recent victims. Clayton says he's already picked out the young hunter he's going to pass the gun along to…but not just yet.

37

The Evolution of a Turkey Hunter

You have to grow as a turkey hunter the same way a child grows to be an adult

For the first 25 or 30 years of my life, my father thought I was irresponsible, irreverent and pretty much a total loss as a contributing member of society – and maybe he wasn't far wrong, at that. I suspect his father, in turn, thought pretty much the same thing about him; from all accounts, Dad was a ring-tailed terror until my Mama got hold of him.

This phenomenon is no recent development. Every generation in the history of the world has thought it was the last one with any sense of maturity and responsibility. Zog the cave man no doubt thought his son was shiftless and without hope of redemption, inclined more toward drawing stick men on the cave walls and flinging rocks at his sister Zogetta than going out to slay a woolly mammoth for winter groceries. But somehow Zog Jr. rose to the occasion, and in his own turn probably wondered if Zog III was ever going to overcome his callowness, shiftlessness and inertia.

The problem, of course, is the so-called generation gap – the age-old phenomenon that causes all adults to be wise and powerful, and all children to be weak and stupid. The gap diminishes with age, and at some point parents and their children usually come together, more or less, on some mutual plane of understanding. This is generally the product of both parties gaining more maturity.

A similar gap exists in turkey hunting. In the beginning, rookie turkey hunters are wide-eyed and eager, like fresh-weaned puppies exploring the big, new world. They charge ahead full-steam, tripping over their own feet and making blunder after blunder. They make too much noise, they call inappropriately, and they seldom seem to learn from their mistakes. Young hunters are much more inclined toward this type of clumsy, unproductive behavior than those who don't come into the sport until they're adults. Also, male hunters seem much more inclined toward it than females. But in almost all rookies, age and gender notwithstanding, this puppyish attitude is present to some degree.

If you're a veteran hunter, and if you remember your beginnings with honesty, you probably recall going through this stage during your own early years in the game. I know I do; I did it in spades. I was as eager and ignorant as they come, and my performance in those first few years showed it. I ran off enough gobblers to stock a medium-sized state, in ways both imaginative and comical.

During this stage, the neophyte hunter is pathetically eager for knowledge, but as we've mentioned, he or she tends to be incapable of absorbing much of it. In those early years, we bounce off one discouraging experience after another, going through turkey hunts like a steel ball through a pinball machine. We react to these knocks, sure, but usually in the wrong direction. We ask questions of experienced hunters, then either forget the answers or ignore them. We gain painful, hard-won field experience and then fail to correctly analyze it or learn from what went wrong.

Some beginning hunters never get past this stage. They struggle along for a few hunts – or a few seasons, depending on their individual capacity for absorbing insult and abuse – and give up in disgust. I was

The Evolution of a Turkey Hunter

The evolution of a turkey hunter, illustrated – Spencer on left, 70-something; son-in-law Blake Moseley center, 40-something; grandson Wyatt Moseley right, 9-something, with Wyatt's first gobbler in 2018. Yes, that's snow.

very nearly one of those to-hell-with-it turkey hunters myself, until a more experienced friend took pity on me toward the end of my fifth season and called up my first gobbler. Read about it in Chapter 34.

It was as I stood over that still-flopping bird that I made the first step in my evolution as a turkey hunter, which is changing from a first-stage beginner to a second-stage beginner. In the first stage, I was pathetically eager to kill a gobbler but didn't really believe it would ever happen. After it did, I was overcome with a bloodlust I find almost impossible to describe. I wanted to kill every gobbler in the state; I wanted turkey blood to run in rivers off the ridges.

It is a fortunate thing for modern-day turkey populations that most turkey hunters are still remarkably inept when they finally manage to kill that first bird and enter the second stage. Otherwise, the carnage would be horrendous. But I was still firmly mired in that ineptitude, so no rivers of blood ran off any of my ridges. I continued to botch one opportunity after another, the only difference being that now I was convinced I could kill those birds. But I was wrong, and my batting average during those next few years proved it.

From conversations with other hunters and from personal observation of many second-stage beginners over the years, I'm convinced my experiences and feelings fall squarely within the norm. This bloodthirsty mindset of most second-stage hunters leads them to push the envelope in their eagerness, even though they still don't know what they're doing and have no business pushing any envelopes whatsoever. The inevitable result is few successful hunts, but many spooked gobblers.

Most novices with a bird or two under their belts continue to follow this pinball style of turkey hunting for another few seasons. As in the first stage of development, some of them never progress beyond this level. Most of this group eventually get discouraged and drop out.

But for those who stick it out, there eventually comes the first glimmering of understanding, which is this: regardless what a turkey hunter thinks about it, a turkey gobbler doesn't have to do *anything*. He doesn't have to come to your calls. He doesn't even have to answer them. Further, he has no set timetable in which to get things done. He can do it tomorrow, or next week. Or never.

Once the novice grasps this concept, he or she enters the third stage of development as a turkey hunter. This stage is what I think of as the "20-bird expert" phase. During this time, which can last anywhere from two or three seasons to a lifetime, the evolving hunter begins to scale back his aggressive push to annihilate every gobbler he hears. He begins to take his cues from the bird, and adjusts his hunting tactics accordingly. If the bird is hot, the hunter will be aggressive. If the bird is henny or seems disinterested or excessively reluctant, the hunter will try different things he hopes will finesse the gobbler into range.

Gradually, the hunter begins to kill a higher percentage of the birds he works. He begins to develop an individual hunting style, and starts feeling less like a complete idiot every time he enters the woods. By the time his tally reaches double digits, the developing hunter has usually reached the faulty conclusion he's pretty good, that he's got this stuff all figured out. This attitude usually lasts for another 10 gobblers or so – hence the term "20-bird expert."

During this stage, which actually represents a regression of sorts, some hunters become absolutely insufferable. When they overhear you telling one of your buddies how a gobbler beat you, they will come over and recite in clear, pear-shaped tones the proper course of action you should have followed to kill the turkey.

These folks begin each hunt with the braggadocio and self-important bearing commonly associated with professional wrestlers. And when they come back to camp both ass-whipped and ass-dragging, (which is much more often than not,) the truth is not in them. They are full of excuses about competition from herds of hens, coyotes spooking their gobblers, interference from other hunters and so on. It is seldom that a 20-bird expert admits he simply made a mistake or that a turkey just plain out-and-out beat him. He always has to lay the blame elsewhere.

Even with this glaring fault, though, the 20-bird expert is inevitably learning more all the while about the craft and craftiness of turkey hunting. Much of this knowledge is subconscious at this point, but still. With each new experience, with each new drubbing, our hunter builds on the foundation of knowledge that begins the day he realizes he can't summon a turkey to the gun through desire and willpower alone. Eventually, this knowledge matures and blossoms into yet another realization – that he can't kill them all, no matter how good he gets.

Nor, he also discovers with no little surprise, does he really want to.

And so the turkey hunter enters the fourth stage of development. He begins to again seek out the advice of others, and this time he actually listens to the answers. He begins to think things through *before* he closes in to do battle with a turkey, rather than blundering into each encounter like a coon dog pup. He tries what he thinks will have the best chance of success, based on his own past experiences and what he has learned from others.

Henny gobbler? Tactic A. Traveling salesman? Tactic B. Bird strutting in the middle of a pasture? Tactic C. He develops more patience when dealing with Bad Birds, but he also acquires the discipline to walk away from an exceptionally difficult gobbler when things go wrong for too long.

In short, he learns that although most gobblers, even Bad Birds, have their weak spots, many are unkillable on certain days or in certain situations. As a result, the hunter doesn't waste as much time trying to kill these super-difficult turkeys. Instead, he spends more time looking for – and finding – more vulnerable gobblers. His success rate further improves, and he starts bringing more birds back to the truck. He doesn't spook as many gobblers as before. The other hunters in his circle begin to think him a pretty good turkey hunter, and in truth, he has become one. Now, instead of avoiding him as they did when he was a 20-bird expert, they begin to seek out his advice. And he gives it, but with much more humility than when he was a 20-bird expert.

Most turkey hunters have this capacity to eventually learn, and if they stick with it long enough, also develop the maturity to be humble. Thus, they eventually reach this fourth evolutionary stage. The time frame is highly variable, and some arrive much quicker than others. Some hunters retain the attitude of a 20-bird expert and never get there at all, even though they may through sheer persistence and the law of averages accumulate a decent collection of turkey beards. There are, after all, suicidal turkeys. Walk enough miles through turkey country and you'll find one now and then.

But most veterans eventually arrive as fourth stage hunters. Most of us stay there, too. The vast majority of turkey hunters, due to the pressing demands of job, family and society in general, can't spare the huge amount of time almost always required for a hunter to progress beyond the "good turkey hunter" fourth-stage category and join the rarefied ranks of the fifth stage – the true experts. Nor, candidly, do most of us have the drive or the mental and physical toughness to spend 40 or 50 days (or more) chasing turkeys across seven or eight states (or more) every spring. That drive, that toughness, is a prerequisite.

Because of the nature of my job, I've had the good fortune to meet and hunt with quite a few folks I'd place in the "expert" category. Usually, these are professional guides or pro-staffers of hunting equipment manufacturers, or both. In other words, people who hunt for a living.

Not all of them, though. I've met many non-professional hunters I'd also have to classify as experts. Regardless of their pro or am status, these folks are confident about their abilities, but modest and humble as well. They know they can kill turkeys with some degree

Most veterans eventually evolve into fourth-stage hunters, if they live long enough and hunt often enough. A few, like my Mississippi friends Dale Causey (left) and Andy Terrell, make it to stage 5.

of consistency, but they also know they're not infallible and they'll continue to make mistakes.

As mentioned, the climb to this top level isn't easy. Nor, generally, is it quick, since it usually requires many years of experience. But if a hunter who's reached the "good" level continues to pay attention, continues to learn from his mistakes and experiences, listens to the advice of others and lives long enough to accumulate enough woods time, he too may finally develop into an expert.

From my standing, somewhere between the 20-bird expert and the good turkey hunter, it's that thought that gives me the most hope.

38

Hunting on the Shady Side of 70

It's still as enjoyable as ever, but some of the urgency has faded

That first turkey hunt is a long time gone, but the memory stands fresh as this morning's biscuits. No need to repeat the details here; see Chapter 34 for that. I didn't kill a bird that morning, but it was on that fateful morning in the late 1970s, when I stood on a ridge not far east of Natchez and listened to seven gobblers sound off one after another, that the trajectory of my life changed.

It took, at most, nine or ten seconds for those seven gobblers to complete their overlapping serenade. In the instant before the racket started, I was not a turkey hunter. By the time the woods were quiet again, I was.

Just. That. Quick.

I didn't know a damned thing about turkey hunting, of course. I was there only because a friend had nagged me to go. I didn't care much for deer hunting, and since I expected turkey hunting to be similar, I didn't think I'd like it, either. But after those gobblers did their thing in that Mississippi dawn, I knew I'd been wrong. By the time that hunt ended, I was firmly, permanently hooked.

In those days, turkey populations were in the early to middle stages of their remarkable comeback. Turkeys weren't even legal game in many states, and even where these big birds were lawfully hunted, it was a new experience. Most of us were still pretty far down the learning curve. There weren't all that many of us back then, either, so the birds were pretty safe. Sure, there were some good turkey men even in those days, but they grew few to the hill and mostly kept their own counsel. They weren't much inclined to offer advice to us newbies.

We found ourselves in a fix: bitten by the bug but not knowing how to scratch. So we attended calling contests and turkey hunting seminars where and when we could find them. We read the few books and magazine articles then available on the subject. And because it's true that misery loves company, we sought out other neophytes who shared both our enthusiasm and our ineptitude. But most important of all, we hunted. At every opportunity, we got out there and embarrassed ourselves in front of turkeys.

Early on, we lurched through turkey hunts like drunken sailors through Singapore. We wallowed in our own ignorance like pigs in slop. We made horrible, comical, disastrous mistakes, then doubled down on them. We called inappropriately and inexpertly. We moved when we shouldn't, and were too scared to move when we should. We changed set-ups too often, or conversely, not often enough. We skylighted ourselves on ridgelines; we blundered into food plots and fields without first checking them for turkeys. In short, we did everything wrong except wave a white flag and holler "Here, turkey turkey turkey!" It wouldn't shock me to learn somebody somewhere even tried that.

Not surprisingly, we ran off turkeys in wholesale numbers, educating far more birds than we killed. But the beauty of the situation was that turkeys were increasing faster than turkey hunters, and there were so many birds and so little competition from other hunters we could afford to make those mistakes. And slowly, gradually, we began to learn.

It was the polar opposite of the situation our fathers and

Hunting on the Shady Side of 70

grandfathers had faced a half-century earlier. In those discouraging days before the cannon net and modern wildlife management, things looked bleak indeed for the future of the wild turkey. In most of the country they'd already been pounded out of existence with the double hammers of habitat destruction and year-round unregulated hunting.

Even where turkeys remained, they were generally so scarce that just hearing a single gobble made it a good hunt. Most of the few remaining turkey hunters were convinced these birds would soon be extinct in the wild. Therefore, they hunted them for the same reason ornithologists and museum curators of that era were shooting ivory-billed woodpeckers: because they wanted a specimen or two for their collections before they were all gone.

When opportunities come that rarely, you learn to hunt

In the bad old days, people hunted turkeys for the same reason museum curators hunted ivory-billed woodpeckers: to secure a specimen for their collections before they were all gone.

conservatively. The common premise during those days of scarcity was that if a turkey answered your call, he'd eventually come looking. You just needed to be patient, give the turkey time to be a turkey, and not get in a rush and do anything that would alert the bird and spook him – such as call more than once or twice an hour. These guys learned to take patience to a new level.

Not me and my fellow neophytes, though. Nosiree Bob. As mentioned, turkey numbers were on a steep upward curve by the time many hunters of my generation got started. Where I hunted, in the Ouachita Mountains of western Arkansas and eastern Oklahoma, it was common to hear a dozen or more gobblers on a given morning. If you stubbed your toe with this one, no problem; go to the one gobbling over thataway. If you messed up on him as well, there was more than likely another one gobbling farther down the ridge.

And so we stumbled along from one gobbler to the next, spooking birds, leaving ranks of educated turkeys in our wake but not taking many of them home. Many (if not most) of my fellow low-information turkey hunters operated in similar fashion through the '70s and '80s. This was partly because we didn't know any other way, and partly because of the video craze that hit the turkey hunting during that time span.

To the best of my knowledge it was Will Primos and my old friend Ronnie "Cuz" Strickland who made the first quality turkey hinting video, called "The Truth About Spring Turkey Hunting." It opened the floodgates. Competing turkey call and camo manufacturers started cranking out exciting, action-packed videos and TV shows. In these on-screen hunts, they (to steal the words Will Primos stole ahead of me) "called too much and called too loud."

The video hunts were exciting and fast-paced, with gobblers and hunters competing to see who could make the most noise. Film-makers soon learned the dead air and long waits that comprise the typical turkey hunt don't make good TV, so they wisely deleted all that stuff. The 45-minute approach of a gobbler in real time translated into 35 seconds on tape, and while we viewers were aware of that fact, these extremely truncated television hunts nevertheless reinforced our run-and-gun hunting mentality. *See?* we told ourselves and each other. *This is the way the pros do it, so it must be right.*

My legs were much younger in those days, and climbing mountains and walking miles through rough country wasn't a problem. My modus operandi was simple, direct and mindless: 1. Cover as much ground as possible. 2. Stop every couple hundred yards and call like a maniac in an attempt to make a turkey gobble.

It wasn't at all uncommon for me to cover six or seven miles on a morning turkey hunt. And yes, I did get a lot of turkeys to gobble, but my success rate on those turkeys was singularly unimpressive. My problem was simple yet profound: I didn't know what to do after I made the turkey gobble.

But I struck a lot of 'em, sure enough, and I'd always sit down and give it my best effort. When it worked it was usually pretty spectacular, with the turkey – sometimes multiple turkeys – charging my position like Gall and Crazy Horse charged Custer. I still managed to screw up most of even these super-hot gobblers by committing some random greenhorn faux pas, moving at the wrong time or whatever, but unfortunately I tagged a few of them, too.

Those infrequent but exciting successes kept me running and gunning for a good many years, and that's why I used "unfortunately" in the preceding paragraph. Every time I managed to kill one of these hormone-addled sophomores (they were usually inexperienced two-year-olds,) it reinforced my faith in those low-percentage hunting tactics. Never mind all the failures. I killed this one, didn't I?

As time went on and the popularity of turkey hunting started catching up to turkey numbers, we run-and-gunners started noticing a change in turkey behavior. By the 1990s, those dozen-gobbler mornings weren't so common any more, and it got harder and harder to strike turkeys with our go-for-broke hunting style. And those we did strike were increasingly more reluctant to approach the aggressive calling. Things had changed.

I didn't, though. Old habits die hard, and I carried on as before, wearing out boots and turkey calls by over-using both. And when one of those increasingly infrequent two-year-olds did come charging in, blowing and stomping, and let me kill him in spite of myself, it made up for a lot of turkey-less mornings.

However, sometimes good fortune comes in disguise, and when I fell off a ledge in April 1994 and tore up my right knee, it slowed me down considerably. It didn't stop me, understand; it was turkey season, and after all it was only a screwed-up knee. So I wrapped it tight and played hurt for the rest of the season, gimping through the woods like Quasimodo in search of a bell rope.

Since I was covering much less territory, I figured lower-key calling would be appropriate as well. Somehow it just seemed logical, so I tried it. And I quickly noticed an increase in the number of gobblers I was making contact with. There was also a definite improvement in my kill percentage. By the time that season was finished, I was a fervent disciple of a new religion.

Nobody has ever accused me of half-assing any of my obsessions, and that held true with this new approach. During the season of 1995, even with a healed knee under me, my rate of progress through the woods made snails look speedy. Where I once covered a half-dozen miles in a morning, I was now traveling a mile or less. Sometimes much less. Moss started growing on the north side of my seldom-used box call. Wrens nested in the pockets of my turkey vest.

Okay, I'm overdrawing it some. But I really had dialed it back, no fooling, and the result was I beat myself. That season was pretty much a bust, and I worked fewer gobblers – and tagged fewer – than I had in several seasons. I'd throttled back too much; I'd turned a poor tactic into a good one and then turned it bad again. I wasn't covering enough ground to locate many gobblers, and I was being too hesitant and wimpy with the few I did find. It was pretty obvious I'd overdone things – or under-done them, depending on how you wanted to look at it. There was a happy medium in there somewhere, if only I could find it.

I've been looking for it ever since. My knee is okay now but other parts of me are going south, and it seems like every day something new starts hurting. I easily outpace all but the peppiest snails nowadays, but I'm no longer what you'd call a run-and-gun hunter. I guess you'd call my hunting style laid-back, or maybe wait-and-see. Something like that. I cover ground but I don't hurry; I call aggressively sometimes but not always; I can wait, if necessary, with the patience of Job, but I

These days, Spencer easily outpaces all but the peppiest snails, but he's no longer what you'd call a run and gun hunter.

can also (usually) walk away from an obstinate turkey and go look for another one.

And I kill some turkeys these days. Not as many as you, maybe, but I tag one every once in a while. Enough over the years, at any rate, to have dampened that desperate hunger for the kill that dominated my early turkey hunting. It hasn't, though, lessened my desire to hear them gobble, to work them close, to converse with them in their own language on their own turf, to bend them to my will. That desire is still as strong as ever, and if that need to get inside their heads ever weakens inside mine, that's when I'll quit.

Don't get me wrong here. The adrenalin rush is still very much there. The sound of a nearby gobble still raises the hair at the back of my neck, and when a turkey approaches my heart still races and my breath comes short. Maybe not quite the way they did early on, but bad enough. Usually in those early years, I had to go behind a tree and lose my breakfast after killing a gobbler. Nowadays, it only happens on every third or fourth bird.

Ironically, it may be this dimming of the burning need to kill them that helps me kill more of them these days. Since the kill isn't as important now as it was then, I'm a little calmer and more collected in the presence of the adversary, and this gives me an edge. Maybe.

It's something to think about, anyway, on those hunts when nothing is happening and my mind starts to drift. I'm more than likely into my last decade as a turkey hunter, and sometimes, toward the end of a particularly grueling season, I think back down the years to that seminal moment when I killed that first gobbler and my life's path took an irreversible swerve. In these moments, I wonder if maybe things might have worked out better had I gone fishing that long-ago April morning instead of caving in to my buddy's nagging and going turkey hunting.

Unquestionably, my life would have worked out simpler. Less

money spent, more spring fishing, maybe a marriage saved somewhere along the way.
	But better?
	Nah.

39

Epitaph for a Turkey Hunter

A partial accounting of a four-decade friendship

He was one of a kind. Big (not fat, just big,) rawboned, sunburned, leathery, John Thomas Aycock was the epitome of a country boy. Except when he was wearing camouflage hunting clothes, and for the last few weeks as he lay on his deathbed, I'm not sure I ever saw him in anything but blue jeans.

Tommy was the epitome of a turkey hunter, too, and he hunted these big, elusive birds with the focused, single-minded intensity of a Hindu penitent. We met in May, 1981, when he walked into the shop of the business where I worked and spied a gobbler tail fan I had recently boraxed and tacked to a board. I'm glad he saw it, because that tail fan launched a friendship that lasted 40 years.

Tommy was already a 20-year veteran of the turkey wars, while I (as proven by the fact that the tail fan mentioned here was from my very first gobbler) was the rankest of beginners. But that made no difference to Tommy; I was a blooded turkey hunter, and that made us brothers in the fraternity, both of us members of the Tenth Legion years before either of us had ever heard of Tom Kelly. In Tommy's direct, to-the-point way of thinking, that made us equals.

What struck me during that first of many, many conversations was the obvious fact that he was as happy that I, a stranger, had killed a gobbler as he would have been about tagging one himself. Soon enough, I learned this was a hard-wired part of his make-up. He was generous with his joy of living and readily extended it to others.

It took us an hour to swap out his oxygen bottle that day, a job that could normally be accomplished in three minutes. It would have taken longer, but my boss came back to the shop and dragged Tommy out of there by the arm.

We shared many varied experiences over our four decades of friendship, most of them involving outdoor stuff: duck, dove, squirrel and deer hunting; bass, trout, bream and catfishing; trapping for mink, beavers, otters, bobcats and other furbearers. But mostly we shared turkey hunts, either in each other's company or vicariously through frequent phone calls during turkey season, as we called each other to brag, commiserate or seek advice on a particularly obstinate turkey. I promise you, I picked his brain about more than one of the Bad Birds in these two books.

We traveled a lot together, mostly chasing turkeys – in Arkansas, Mississippi, Missouri, Oklahoma and Kansas – and we shared many experiences, both good and bad. Some of our hunts had elements of both. Like this one:

We were in the Devil's Backbone Wilderness Area in southern Missouri. Back then, in the late 1980s when our legs and lungs were younger, it was our favorite place to hunt. We got on a stubborn late-morning bird and finally got him coming. It was Tommy's shot, but as the gobbler closed the distance he slid off to the right, forcing Tommy to shoot left-handed.

If you've ever shot off your wrong shoulder, you know how awkward it feels. That's why Tommy wanted the bird to be standing still for the shot. But the dang turkey kept walking to the right, and Tommy kept corkscrewing farther and farther around his tree, and it was about to become impossible. Panic in his voice, he stage-whispered, "Make him stop!" I clucked sharply on my box call, and in the next half-second, three things happened: The gobbler stopped walking. He ran his head up. And Tommy killed him.

I jumped up and started running to the bird, the way we used to do before souped-up turkey loads and heavier-than-lead shot made it pretty much unnecessary. After a few steps I realized I was running by myself. I stopped, looked back and saw Tommy on all fours, blood pouring out of his nose onto the leaves. He'd had the gun so far to the right his left thumb was on the right side of his nose, and the recoil of

Tommy Aycock, happy but still a little addled, a few minutes after killing a turkey and breaking his nose.

the big 12 gauge broke his schnozz as efficiently as a fastball.

"You all right?" I asked.

"Yeah. Go get my turkey." It was a reasonable request; the gobbler was thundering around out there in a tight circle, beating the forest floor with both wings. So I ran a few more steps and turned around again. Tommy was struggling up on one knee, leaning on his shotgun, blood still pouring out of his nose but now onto the front of his shirt.

"You sure you're all right?"

"Yes! Go get my damn turkey."

So I went and got his damn turkey. By the time we got back to the truck he looked like a gladiator who'd been playing for the losing team. There was human blood all over the front of his clothes and turkey blood all down his back. "It's worth it," he said. "I'll do it all over again if I ever get the chance."

In case you don't recognize it, that's turkey hunting dedication right there. It gripped this man like horsehide grips a baseball.

Another time, we were camping and hunting in the Ouachita Mountains of western Arkansas, not far from Mt. Ida. To call this a poor-boy camp would be an understatement. We had a tent, two sleeping bags, one Coleman lantern, a black skillet, two or three bent forks, a spatula, a coffee pot, two chipped coffee mugs, an ice chest, a five-gallon water cannister, two rickety folding camp chairs and a roll of toilet paper. Our provisions consisted of a loaf of bread, a dozen eggs, a pound of bacon, five pounds of potatoes, a package of bologna, some rat-trap cheese, a salt shaker and a little can of coffee. That was our entire string.

But it was enough. We were tough and poor and still young enough to stand it, and neither of us had enough sense to realize we were roughing it. We were, after all, sleeping smack in the middle of the turkey woods. What more could you want?

First day, nothing. The second morning, we hiked up the ridge behind camp. At the top, Tommy went east and I went west. About 9 a.m. I heard a shot back in his direction, and I figured he'd killed one. Okay, good. Turkey breast and taters for supper. After a while I moseyed back that way, and down in a little ravine about where we'd split up I saw a dead turkey. Fresh. A hen.

I figured Tommy had killed it by accident, maybe shooting at a gobbler. It happens. I left her where I found her, and when I got back to camp Tommy jumped me about it.

"Why'd you kill that hen?" He'd seen her laying there, too, and had left her the same as I had.

I denied it and accused him of doing the deed, and he denied it, too. I believed him then and believe him now. Tommy would lie about turkey hunting as quick as the next guy, but we didn't lie to each other about it. The only explanation we could come up with was that some other hunter had got in between us, shot the hen and left her.

Sitting in camp eating dry bologna and cheese sandwiches, we got to thinking about that hen turkey up there going to waste. I have already mentioned we were in a bare-bones camp, broke as the Ten Commandments, and in the end, practicality won out over legality. We went back up the mountain, ran a red-shouldered hawk off the hen and breasted her out on the spot. Then we guiltily snuck the meat back to camp and cooked her for supper that night. All the while we were nervous as first-time bank robbers, certain we were going to get caught any minute. But we didn't, and the statute of limitations has long since run out so I can safely tell you about it.

She was delicious.

Tommy Aycock was more than just a good, dedicated hunter and outdoorsman. He was a master rice and soybean farmer, for one thing, one of the best in Arkansas. He was a family man to beat all family men. He was also the kindest, gentlest, most generous, most thoughtful man I've ever known. He was a gentleman in the truest sense of the word – a gentle man. We were friends 40 years, and I

John Thomas "Tommy" Aycock was more than just a good, dedicated hunter and outdoorsman. He was also a gentleman, in the truest sense of the word – a gentle man.

got 40 birthday cards from him. If he'd lived another month, I'd have gotten another one. It shames me to say that I failed to reciprocate, but it never occurred to Tommy to feel slighted by it. He was about giving, not taking.

Tommy was fiercely loyal to his friends, and I guess if he had any enemies he was loyal to them as well. But I honestly couldn't tell you if he had enemies or not. If he did, he never mentioned them to me. Matter of fact, I never heard him say a truly bad thing about anybody.

He was a highly moral man, and – not that I think drinking is immoral, mind you – he never was a drinker. The only alcohol I ever saw him consume was red wine, which he drank for a while when one of his doctors told him an ounce or two of the stuff every night before bedtime would be good for his heart or his red blood cell count or his insomnia or something. There for a year or two he always had a bottle of dago red with him. It was both comical and entertaining to watch him screw up his face and choke down that little glass of nightly wine.

By the same token, it would have been comical to watch him that afternoon in about 2004 or 2005, when we were hunting near where Jill and I live in the north Arkansas Ozarks. Staying in our small guest house, Tommy got a plastic bottle out of the refrigerator to carry on an afternoon hunt. He thought it held water, but instead for some now-forgotten reason contained gin put there by my wife. It was a warm late-April day and Tommy walked quite a distance to get to his chosen hunting spot, and by the time he got there he'd worked up a thirst. Out came the "water" bottle, and he took a couple healthy chugs before realizing something was dreadfully, horribly wrong.

That evening after we all got back to the house, Tommy told me where my "water" bottle was, and what I could do with it when I found it. He said he blew every turkey out of that section of woods with his coughing and gagging and choking, and he thought he was going to die before he got things back under control.

I thought it was hilarious. Tommy failed to share that opinion. After giving me the cussing of my life (moral he was, anti-profanity he was not,) he accused me of setting a booby trap for him. But I didn't, I swear. Not that I'm above stuff like that, but I just didn't think of it. Anyway, none of my practical jokes ever work out that well.

Aside from that one thing he didn't find so funny, though, Tommy had a keen sense of humor. He loved a good joke, and – again, aside from the one thing – if the joke was on him, so much the better.

But his last good joke, as it turned out, was on me. Not long after the 2019 turkey season I visited Tommy in the hospital, only a month or so before he died. I told him I'd gone back to the Devil's Backbone that spring on a turkey hunt, and I'd passed by the spot where he'd broken his nose. I told him it was going to be my last trip, though, because the landscape was just too rough for old men.

A little smile flirted with the corners of his mouth. "Oh, you never know," he said. "You might go there again someday." I should have smelled a rat, but I didn't. Not right then.

A few weeks later, when Tommy's daughter-in-law Elizabeth called to tell me his time was about used up, she also told me he had two requests for me and wanted to let me know what they were ahead of time, so I wouldn't be blindsided. Suddenly I caught a whiff of that rat.

One of the requests was that I do a eulogy at his memorial service. It was an honor to be asked, and I accepted gladly and, I think, did it fairly well when the time came. Parts of that eulogy have been included in this chapter.

The other request was Tommy's final joke. He wanted me to scatter his ashes. Guess where?

So, he was right and I was wrong. I will indeed be making one more trip to the Devil's Backbone. Let me tell you exactly what that entails:

First, you somehow get yourself to West Plains, in southern

Missouri. Then you take a narrow farm-to-market road about 20 miles west and turn off that on a bumpy gravel road that hasn't seen much maintenance since the Reagan administration. Take that road to its end, about 5 or 6 miles, and park at the sign at the wilderness boundary sign that says "No vehicles beyond this point." Then lace up your most comfortable hiking boots, and don't forget your water bottle because you're going to need it. (Check to make sure it's water, ha ha.)

Then you start walking. And you walk. And you walk some more. And then you climb some, and go down in holes some, and climb back out of them. Then, to finally get out on the Backbone itself (a narrow spine of granite and rotten limestone surrounded by thin air and soaring buzzards,) you have to go down a steep 300-foot slope covered with baseball-sized rocks that like to roll under your feet and try to break your ankles. Finally, four rough miles from the truck, you're there. You're on the Devil's Backbone. Then you have to do all that in reverse to get back to your ride.

I gotta hand it to you, Tommy, that was a good one. *"Oh, you never know. You might go there again someday."* No wonder you were grinning; I bet it took considerable effort to keep from laughing out loud. At least you didn't saddle me with a chore like Gus McCrae hung on Woodrow Call. I don't have to lug you from Montana to Texas in a buckboard wagon and bury you in a grove of pecan trees. That's something, I guess.

As fate and the calendar would have it, about the time this book comes back from the printer I'll be making that trek to the Backbone to carry out one of my friend's final requests. Difficult as it's going to be (in more ways than one,) that too will be an honor.

Tommy Aycock died on a hot, beautiful summer Sunday in 2019, just shy of his 82nd birthday. Jill and I were leaving a convention in Springfield, Missouri when the news came. We were just south of town, headed for Russellville, Arkansas to tell Tommy goodbye, when my phone chirped. It was a text message from Elizabeth telling us we were too late. My amigo had chased his last gobbler.

It's an established fact that big ol' rough he-man turkey hunters don't cry. A couple minutes later I was driving along, being a big ol' rough he-man turkey hunter, wiping at the dust or grit or whatever it was in the truck that was making my peepers water, when out of the corner of my eye I glimpsed a black blob in a field.

This next is God's truth. You can't make this stuff up.

When I saw the black blob it looked familiar, and hunter's instinct took over. I jerked my head to the right and focused on a mature gobbler in full strut, 50 yards off the highway. Just as I made him out as a turkey he ran his neck out and double-gobbled, and just that quick we were past him.

I couldn't hear it, of course. We were driving fast, the windows were up and the air conditioner was blowing a hurricane. But I didn't need to hear it. I knew what it sounded like.

I bet Tommy heard it, though, and when I saw that big gobbler send that double-barreled salute to my old friend, I knew things were all right. Things were as they should be. Tommy wasn't uncomfortable or in pain any more, and he had his strength and his youth back after several years of failing health. He was on his way to a place where the turkeys gobble every day, and the fish are always biting.

Additionally, I knew one day soon I'd be making one more trip to our favorite hunting place with my old friend.

Thank you for that, Tommy. I'll see you on the Backbone.

40

The Gift Bird

**Some turkeys are more important than others.
This one was as important as they get.**

There wasn't a turkey gobbling anywhere as I moseyed toward the log landing where Jill and I had agreed to rendezvous at 9 a.m. We'd selected the spot because it was convenient, because we could both reach it with no problem from the widely-spaced places from which we'd started at dawn, and because it was a good place from which to launch a mid-morning, Plan B hunt.

Easing through the greening woods, I thought about how fortunate I was to be sharing this hunt with my favorite hunting partner on this fine April morning. Six months earlier, the odds both of us would be here hovered somewhere between slim and none…

* * *

"Jim, this is Connie, Dr. Wright's nurse," came the voice through the phone. "I don't want to scare you, but you need to bring Jill to the clinic immediately. Don't let her drive. Stop at the drug store on the way and pick up the prescription I've called in. Have her take the pill immediately, in the pharmacy parking lot, and come from there straight to the clinic. Please do it *right now*."

Maybe Connie wasn't trying to scare me, but she did it anyway. Not that I hadn't been expecting something. For several months, there'd been a gradual but profound change in my wife – a steady decline in her normally boundless curiosity and energy, substantial weight gain, a noticeable lack of enthusiasm for the outdoor lifestyle we both loved so much. A lack of enthusiasm for everything else, for that matter. I'd always admired Jill's work ethic and punctuality regarding writing assignments and deadlines, but recently those had been slipping, too. For the first time since I'd known her, she was missing deadlines and giving editors less than her best work.

But the most alarming thing was her increasing difficulty with short-term memory. "What do you want for supper tonight?" she'd ask, sitting down with her morning coffee. We'd decide on that evening's menu. Before her cup was empty, she'd say, "What do you want for supper tonight?"

I tried to convince myself these were normal functions of aging. After all, we were both pushing 60 at the time, and Father Time is cruel. We all get older, heavier and lazier – or at least I do. But that memory thing was worrisome, and I nagged Jill until she made a doctor's appointment.

After her private appointment with the doctor, I asked for a consultation. When I told him about Jill's increasing memory lapses and recent loss of vitality, he was concerned enough to schedule an MRI the following morning, Tuesday.

Bright and early Wednesday, I held the phone and heard the controlled urgency in the nurse's voice.

* * *

"I know you're not a trained radiologist, but that's not required here," Dr. Wright said when we arrived at the clinic and were ushered immediately to his office. The MRI film showed an image of Jill's head from above, and square in the center front of her cranium was an oval tumor the size of a turkey egg. I am not exaggerating; I can show you the damn film. And the doctor was right. An imbecile could have read it.

My memory of the next couple hours is hazy. Through the blur and buzz of incipient panic, I heard Dr. Wright telling us Springfield and Little Rock both had excellent neurosurgery units. I needed to take Jill to one or the other immediately, he said, while he handled the arrangements as we made the two-hour trip. He said he could arrange for an ambulance, but that would take time and he thought I'd be able to deliver her faster. And time, he said, was of the essence.

"Don't go home to pack," he said, handing me the MRI envelope and ushering us to the door. "Don't stop for lunch. Don't get stupid and have a wreck, but drive as fast as you're comfortable with. She needs to be there yesterday." The one-pill prescription, he said, was a potent anti-seizure drug, and though he didn't say it, he was obviously thinking Jill should be in convulsions already.

Jill and I talked during the drive to Little Rock, but I couldn't begin to tell you what we said. The only thing I distinctly remember is my wife, who could die or start having seizures at any minute, doing her best to put my mind at ease. "I'm going to be fine," she said again and again, reaching across to pat my arm. "Everything's going to be okay."

Flashers winking vigorously, we arrived at the hospital's emergency room entrance at 10:30 a.m. A nurse was waiting for us with a wheelchair. At 1 p.m. my wife went into surgery, and I went into a tailspin.

* * *

Depending on context and situation, a minute can pass in the blink of an eye or last a lifetime. Jill was under the surgeon's knife for 20 hours. Every one of those 1200 minutes was a lifetime, and only the calming presence of our daughter Leslie, who sat beside me almost the

The author has taken his share of gobblers over the years, but the one he was about to face would be the most important of his life.

whole time, got me through. The only good news in that 1200 lifetimes was the information a scrub nurse brought out – that the tumor wasn't malignant.

But of course, I wasn't the one who had it rough. While I sat in relative comfort in a hospital waiting room, Jill was on a surgeon's table with her head cut open. She was unconscious through the ordeal, naturally, but still it was her, not me, who had a big slice of her skull sawed loose and laid down over her face like a wedge of cantaloupe, while the neurosurgeon used a laser to carefully separate the huge tumor from the delicate tissues of her frontal lobes.

To be brief: Jill survived the ordeal. You already knew that, but here's something you don't know. When they let me into recovery, where Jill was still coming out of anesthesia, I could see in her eyes she was already back. Still groggy, black-eyed as a raccoon, wearing a turbanesque bandage that looked like Marge Simpson's hairdo, she gave me a woozy grin and a wink. "Told you I'd be okay," she said.

And just that quick, I was, too.

Jill came out of surgery on Thursday morning. On the following Thursday I brought her home – appropriately, on Thanksgiving Day.

Her work ethic and sense of responsibility resurfaced, and so did her love of living. She quickly got back in good graces with her editors, and she started an exercise regime that still astounds me. You'd have thought she was training for the Olympics. She walked, jogged, dieted, exercised – not making a fuss about it, just doing it – and the pounds melted away. She still refuses to let me tell anyone the numbers, but you wouldn't believe it anyway. What's impressive, though, is this: between Thanksgiving and April she lost every pound she'd gained, plus a few more. By the time turkey season opened, she was her old self – slim, trim and in considerably better shape than her husband.

* * *

My morning hunt had been unproductive. As already mentioned, we'd started our morning hunt from different places so we could challenge different gobblers – Jill to hunt a bird she'd worked the day before, me to try for one that had been gobbling near the lake.

My bird was near the lake, all right, but on the wrong side of it. By the time I got to the water and figured it out, he'd flown down and shut up. Except for Jill's gobbler, which I could just barely hear, no other turkeys were gobbling within earshot. She told me later that when her bird flew down it walked away from her, passing near the spot where we'd agreed to rendezvous. Then it also shut up.

Hunts like that are par for the course, especially on the public lands we usually hunt. After Jill's gobbler got quiet, I went on a roundabout through some pretty good country, trying to find a turkey to play with.

I didn't find one, though, and about 8:30 I started moving toward our pre-established meeting spot. Jill was already there, reading a book and wearing a smug look. A very nice gobbler lay on the ground beside her. We quietly bantered for a few minutes, like hunting partners do:

"Who gave you that turkey, girlie?"

"Whassa matter, big boy, can't you find a turkey to shoot?"

"I save my tags for big turkeys. But that's a fat one for such a little bitty guy, ain't it?"

After that and more trash talk, we decided to go north, where we'd heard several birds gobbling the previous day. But we couldn't get anything going, and with Missouri's 1 p.m. curfew approaching, we decided to drive to a nearby spot that sometimes held a midday gobbler.

We stopped just short of the truck to make one last call. It's a little ritual we nearly always repeat, and on occasion it pays off. First I yelped on my Lohman box and got no response. I gave Jill an exaggerated, now-it's-your-turn finger roll, and when she hit her higher-pitched Black Mystik box a gobbler cut her off. He was close, but not so close we panicked.

He was in a shady little draw south of the truck. We angled downhill to his level, then closed the gap another 30 yards. I set up out front with Jill 15 yards back, and she raked another series of yelps off the top of her box call. The turkey gobbled hard.

But he seemed content to stay where he was, and presently the clock started becoming a factor. We were running out of it. Jill cranked up the excitement and tempo, trying to force the play, but that trick worked the same way it usually does, which is to say it didn't work at all. The gobbler was singularly unimpressed and wouldn't answer the insistent stuff.

But another gobbler did. This one sounded like he was gobbling

The Gift Bird

from the bed of our truck, less than 250 yards away. When Jill turned loose with the excited stuff, he started our way immediately. Then a third gobbler cranked up from somewhere past the truck, and that one started toward us as well. Then another one started gobbling on private land across a nearby county road, maybe 250 yards away. We didn't figure this one would cross the road and join the party, but he was noisy and he got everybody else stirred up. Finally, as if four weren't enough, another gobbler came in silently behind Jill – I didn't know this until later – and started drumming nonstop, practically in her ear.

Rags to riches. From nothing a scant few minutes ago, we were now hip-deep in interested gobblers.

I already had my gun shouldered, but in my haste I'd forgotten to stick a diaphragm call in my mouth. Now it was too late; I was handcuffed. The closest turkey was *right there,* killable if he'd stick his head up, or take a few steps uphill, or something. The by-the-truck gobbler was steadily getting closer, as was the one just behind him. Jill told me later the drumming turkey was getting closer, too.

That's when the thought hit me like a fist: whichever of these gobblers showed up first was going to be the most significant turkey of my life. Here I was, sitting in front of a woman who just five months before had been at death's door. Following an ordeal most of us can't begin to imagine, she had without complaint fought her way back to health. Now, after calling in and killing a fine gobbler for herself earlier that morning, she was attempting to call in another one for her husband, who already thought she was Wonder Woman.

It's always important to do things right when a turkey is under the gun. The hunt is about much more than the kill, true enough, but the kill is still pretty important. You don't want to screw it up at the moment of truth, assuming that moment arrives. But this kill was so far beyond important it was off the chart. I absolutely *had* to get this one right.

You think you know something about pressure? Think again.

I'm normally pretty cool when a gobbler is coming. Sure, my pulse races and the adrenaline courses, but I can usually keep myself under control, if not quite calm, until the gobbler is down and I'm standing on its head. Only then do I get the shakes and the heebie-jeebies.

Not this time. As soon as I realized how momentous this turkey was, I broke into a drenching sweat and became a quivering mess. My gun barrel, until then steady as a rock, gyrated like a coochie dancer on speed. The turkey in front of me gobbled again, and my quivering ramped up another notch.

Those lifetime-long minutes that had tortured me in the waiting room were gone, and in their place on this hunt were the blink-of-an-eye kind. I knew quitting time was perilously close, but I couldn't look at my watch.

The turkey held his ground. Finally, with only a few minutes left, Jill changed her calling strategy. Ignoring the hung-up gobbler in front of us, she started conversing with the gabby one across the road. When the close turkey would gobble she did nothing, but every time the private land bird said anything she was all over him with yelps, cutts and excited clucks.

It drove the nearest bird nuts. After Jill ignored him the fourth or fifth time, he took a few steps up the hill and suddenly there he was, all of him, searching suspiciously for the fickle hen.

When things are that important, they become easy. The sight of the gobbler calmed me instantly, and my cosmic case of the yips vanished. The gun barrel quit waving, and I put the bead on the line where wattles met neck feathers. When he ran his head up for a better look, I uncapped it for him. He collapsed, and before I got up to claim him I glanced at my Indiglo. Six minutes of hunting time remained.

I'd killed quite a few gobblers before that day, and I've killed a bunch since. But none of them compare with that one, nor will I ever kill one that does. He wasn't a bad turkey – 22 pounds, ten-inch beard, one-inch spurs if I fibbed a smidgen. Not as good as Jill's bird, but still a good one. But he could have weighed 13 or 30, could have had a nubbin beard or a bell rope, could have had no spurs at all or two-inch hay hooks, and none of it would have made any difference. None of it would have changed the way I felt.

Because this one, this most important gobbler I will ever shoot, was a present from my hunting partner.

And also a present from God.

That's me on the right with The Gift Bird, and Jill on the left with her "little bitty guy." Two lucky hunters, in more ways than one.

Epilogue

Where Do We Go From Here?

I don't want to turn this book into a downer. But if turkey hunting is to stay as good as it's been, there are things that need saying and things we must do. What follows here is my personal opinion. Call it a guess; that's equally accurate. But it's an educated guess, based on more than four decades of watching and studying turkeys and turkey hunting, and it's shared in whole or part by a lot of experienced turkey hunters I know and respect. Accept all, part or none of it, as you wish. But something is happening out there in turkey country, and we need to get a handle on it.

My life has been enriched by the pursuit of wild turkeys. Yours too, probably. Why else would you be reading this book?

Of course, these same wild turkeys have also made our lives more complicated, aggravating, frustrating and expensive. They've caused us to alienate bosses; inconvenience friends and family; lose crops, jobs and wives; miss Sunday services; make deceitful excuses to practically every non-turkey hunter we know; travel far too much; buy equipment we don't need; put too much wear and tear on our trucks, boots and joints; and more. Much more. For me, the pursuit of turkeys has given me an uncommon way to eke out a living – by going out and getting my butt handed to me by dozens of these super-wary birds each spring, then coming home and writing about the innovative ways they beat me.

But mostly, wild turkeys have enriched us. Two of my biggest regrets are that I was well into my 30th year before I started hunting them, and well into my 34th before I killed one. Before that first morning in the turkey woods in 1978, I thought in my blissful ignorance that spring mornings were for fishing. Silly me. My opinion now is that I pretty much wasted 20 Aprils and an equal number of Mays before I learned what those two months were really invented for.

* * *

All turkey hunters are at least passingly familiar with the comeback story of the American wild turkey. Thumbnail: For more than 50 years, from the late 1800s to about 1950, common wisdom held that wild turkey populations were doomed to extinction. Turkeys were scarce, turkey hunters even scarcer, and it seemed that the slide was irreversible.

But then along came the cannon net, and about that same time biologists began to get a grip on what habitat conditions turkeys needed for survival. Thanks to the trap-and-transfer efforts of a bunch of dedicated and motivated field biologists, combined with the enactment of more appropriate hunting regulations and better wildlife management practices, things turned around. Turkey numbers rose meteorically, and from a nationwide population estimated to be as low as 30,000, by the end of the 20th century we had something approaching 7 million turkeys from coast to coast and border to border. Maybe a few more. Turkeys were legal game in every state except Alaska.

More recently, however, beginning somewhere around 2005 to 2010, there's been a change for the worse. That meteoric rise in turkey numbers has given way to a substantial decrease in many parts of the country. Wild animals don't hold still and are therefore hard to count, but most turkey biologists agree that as of 2020, when this was written, we're down to somewhere around 6 million birds nationwide, and maybe fewer than that.

That's still a lot of turkeys, but the trend is troubling. Maybe

Epilogue

If we are to have turkeys for tomorrow, we need to make changes today.

(doubtful, but maybe) this is simply one of those down cycles that periodically happen to all wildlife species, especially gallinaceous birds like grouse and turkeys. Maybe (much more likely) it's the inevitable population reduction that results from several consecutive years of wet springs and poor hatches, which many states have experienced lately. Maybe (and I hope it's not this,) we've simply reached and exceeded our nationwide carrying capacity for turkeys, and things are settling back to where, biologically speaking, they need to be.

Whatever the reason or reasons, it's happening. Unless the trend stops on its own or we figure out a way to stop it, books like this one will become scarce as turkey teeth.

Because, see, this book is a collection of outdoor adventures with only one thing in common: intimate interaction between a single hunter – me – and a whole heap of individual wild turkeys. Without good turkey populations, it won't be possible for future turkey hunters (and future turkey writers) to accumulate enough interactions with gobblers to build a book of memories like this.

Don't believe it can happen? Consider: How many new quail hunting books have you read lately that weren't collections of older works, bearing names like "The Best of…" or "A Century of Quail Writing" or something similar? You can't think of many, can you? Know why? *Because there ain't no damn quail anymore!*

Granted, this book's subject matter is a 20-pound bird that can swallow a hickory nut whole and then grind it to powder in his gizzard, not a runty little thing that has to fill up on ragweed seeds to weigh nine ounces. Still, you can draw parallels. Both are, after all, ground-nesting birds. If the quail population can be decimated – and that's a gross understatement in most former quail strongholds – it can happen to turkeys, too. In fact, it's already happened once. We brought them back from the brink 70 years ago, and it looks like we might have to intervene once again.

Epilogue

* * *

My friend Gary Sefton, no slouch himself when it comes to turkey encounters, very aptly and very succinctly summed up the wild turkey in the title of his book: *Lessons Learned From The Magnificent Bird.*

Sefton is an award-winning songwriter – Chris LeDoux, Waylon Jennings, Tom T. Hall, John Anderson and many, many more have recorded his stuff – so he's used to making his point in few words. And he hit one out of the park with that book title.

The Magnificent Bird, indeed. Magnificent enough that we need to sit up and take notice of this recent reversal in turkey populations, and start doing things to reverse the reversal.

Toward that end, shortly after the disappointing 2020 spring turkey season (disappointing for Jill and me, anyway,) I attended a weekend gathering of veteran, weather-beaten, hard-core turkey hunters. We met at a storied hunting lodge in the Black Belt of Alabama, for the express purpose of discussing this disturbing phenomenon. There were twelve of us, and we brought more than 500 years of spring turkey hunting experience and observation to the table.

Part of our reason for gathering was purely social. Most of us have known each other forever, so this was a reunion of sorts. We had a crawfish boil, a fish fry and lots of do-you-remember-when bull sessions that lasted into the wee hours both nights.

But we reserved Saturday afternoon for a serious round-table discussion of the turkey downturn. We've all been watching with growing alarm as the situation has deteriorated over the past decade or so, and from the beginning of our discussion it was evident we'd all been pondering the issue. Although opinions varied as to the causes of the problem, we were on the same page in agreeing we needed to do *something*. Here are a few of the factors tossed around in that long discussion:

Habitat degradation

Many organizations and agencies provide technical assistance, advice and even cost-sharing for farmers and other landowners who want to improve wildlife habitat on their acreage. The Conservation Reserve Program has been a blessing, reclaiming millions of acres of marginal cropland and replacing row crops with prairie, woodlands and wetlands. Acres for Wildlife, a nationwide program administered by state wildlife agencies, has for decades furnished seed, technical advice and on-the-ground assistance to landowners who want to improve wildlife habitat. Private organizations like Quail Unlimited, Delta Waterfowl, Pheasants Forever, Ducks Unlimited and of course the National Wild Turkey Federation have also done their part to restore, protect and improve wild places.

There's no shortage of groups like this who are willing and able to step up to the plate and help. The problem, though, is finding enough landowners willing to make it happen. Farmers understandably don't want to take valuable cropland out of production, and other types of landowners don't want to go to the trouble or expense required to turn poor habitat into good.

Another insidious factor is the fact that nobody is making any more land, and urban sprawl continues to gobble up wild places. Not to pick on anybody, but every time a new Walmart goes up at the edge of town, another 20 acres of dirt is permanently covered with concrete and asphalt. Once that happens, it's gone forever as potential living space for a deer or a dickeybird, a goose or a gobbler.

A few dozen new Walmarts a year might not sound like much, compared to the vastness of the United States. But throw in the thousands of Dollar Generals that have sprung up across rural America in the past decade, add in the highway bypasses, cloverleafs and such that are being built or enlarged to accommodate a growing human population, toss in the many sprawling subdivisions of cookie-

Epilogue

cutter homes being built all over the country to accommodate folks fleeing city life, and top it all off with the new mega-grocery stores and shopping malls cropping up every year to service these suburban communities, and habitat loss becomes significant in a hurry. The death of ten thousand cuts, landscape version.

Nothing we can do about it, I guess, except maybe screw up the economy so badly all commerce ceases. But then, where would we buy our camo and shotguns and turkey ammo, and where would we buy gas so we could go turkey hunting? And where would we get the money in the first place?

It's a head-scratcher, all right. But it's still a problem.

Poor hatches

As mentioned earlier in this rant, the five or six bad hatch years that preceded 2020 have really put the whammy on turkeys. This is especially true in the southeast and Midwest. The ultimate cause has been wet, cool springs, and there's not much we can do about the weather.

But there's also a penultimate cause, and that one we do have some control over. Stepping up efforts to provide optimum nesting cover – *properly interspersed* optimum nesting cover, that is – would go a long way to help hen turkeys protect their nests and poults from rain. A hay field might offer good concealment from predators, but it's doesn't do much to help a hen keep a brood of chicks dry in a thunderstorm. The sad fact is, hay fields are exactly where a large percentage of turkey hens nest these days. It's not optimum, it's just the best thing they have to work with. And even though they may be relatively safe from predators, many nests are destroyed each year as farmers cut hay in May and June.

Scattering a dozen five-acre blackberry, sumac or honeysuckle thickets – or any similar plant that has leaves – throughout a square mile of otherwise decent turkey country would go a long way to mitigate the negative effects of a cold, wet spring.

Predation

This one ties into the "good habitat" factor above. Predation is seldom a problem in excellent habitat, but when habitat is less than ideal, predation becomes a significant factor.

And that fact has been amplified by recent events in the international fur market, which pretty much imploded in 2013. Trapping activity, never a real big thing in the first place, fell off dramatically. Most trappers say they don't trap for the money, and that's true as far as it goes. But if there's no market for your catch, then what?

Using myself as an example, I trapped from 2003 to 2013 with another old river rat named Bill Bradbury. We ran a multi-species line on a large river and a large Corps of Engineers lake. In those days of

Researchers have learned that no age class of turkeys is safe from predation. Great horned owls are perfectly capable of taking down and killing even big old rope-draggers like this one.

good fur prices, half our season's coon catch would pay our expenses. The rest of the coons and all the other stuff we caught – bobcats, otters, mink, muskrats, coyotes, red and gray foxes, even skunks and possums – represented our profit margin.

We didn't get rich, but the money was good enough to make us work a little harder at something we already enjoyed. Who doesn't get a kick out of making money doing something you love?

But more to the point, trapping in those days was profitable enough to lure other folks out there. Bill and I, as mentioned, worked fairly hard at it. Most days we were busy from first light until after sundown, checking traps, making new sets and skinning, fleshing and stretching our catch.

For a decade and a year we put up an impressive pile of fur each season. In 10 weeks we'd typically catch, in addition to the water-based furbearers that aren't a threat to turkeys, 350 to 450 coons, about 100 to 125 assorted foxes, coyotes and bobcats, and who knows how many possums and skunks. Thousands, it seemed like.

That's a lot of egg and poult eaters. Combined with the efforts of the 20 to 30 other trappers working our general area, we pretty much kept land-bound turkey predators in check.

In contrast, last winter my wife Jill Easton and I trapped for a total of 18 days, targeting upland predators (gray fox, bobcat and coyote) in the vast chunk of national forest that surrounds our rural home. We didn't hit it very hard, and were usually back home by noon and had the day's catch skinned, fleshed and on the boards by 2 p.m.

We caught 70-odd cats, coyotes and foxes, plus a pretty good pile of coons, possums and skunks. In those 18 days, we never saw another trapper or saw any sign of one. I'm pretty sure we were the only trappers in our 170,000-acre chunk of national forest last year.

Compare that with the numbers Bill and I used to put up. Then, factor in the catches not made by those other 20 to 30 trappers who sat it out because there wasn't a viable fur market. Expand that

Due to low fur prices and other sociological factors, participation in trapping has fallen to a small fraction of the activity level prior to 2013, when the global fur market collapsed. More egg and poult-eaters looking for groceries means fewer turkeys on the ground.

nationwide and you begin to understand the negative impact on an already-struggling turkey population.

Sure, turkeys have co-existed with predators since they first evolved 11 million years ago. They're not going to go extinct because fur trapping has virtually ceased. But an increased predator load is a significant factor, especially when piled on the other things discussed here.

Poor habitat, for instance. It's a lot easier for a fox or coon (or a snake or a crow or a packrat) to find a turkey nest in a fence row than it is for that same egg-eater to find a nest in one of those five-acre blackberry/sumac patches we talked about earlier.

Epilogue

Correctable or avoidable human factors

Inappropriate controlled burning. Spring/summer burning is becoming more and more popular, on state, federal and large corporate woodlands, and I don't care what today's armchair biologists try to tell you about it, starting fires when ground-nesting birds are still laying and/or incubating is just plain stupid.

Another aggravating factor is the size of these burns. Sure, I'm a capitalist and I understand the economics of scale. I get it that it's a lot cheaper, on a cost-per-acre basis, to burn a 5,000-acre block of timber than it is to burn 10 separate 500-acre blocks. Likewise, it's faster and cheaper to use a helicopter to scatter small incendiary bombs (known as "ping-pong balls" to professional foresters and wildlifers) over the whole area at once than it is to use feet on the ground and drip torches.

But what are we trying to accomplish by burning? Is the objective to do the job as cheaply as possible, or to do it well? If reduction of ground-level fuel is the only objective, fine, send in the helicopter and set a dozen square miles of woods on fire all at once. And do it any time of year that's convenient.

But if you want to improve conditions for wildlife as well as reduce the fuel load, some degree of compromise is in order. Smaller burns are much more wildlife-friendly than great big ones. A backfire moving slowly across the woods gives critters time to get out of the way, as opposed to carpet-bombing the woods with walnut-sized firestarters that can completely surround critters and give them nowhere to flee. And for Pete's sake, lay off burning during nesting season.

Not burning at all. This one's almost as bad as inappropriate burning; it just takes longer for the effects to show. Mostly this is a problem on private land, where the outdated concept of complete fire suppression is still practiced by many landowners. This leads to several undesirable things. Fuel buildup is one, because it increases the likelihood of a devasting wildfire somewhere down the line. Think about the chapparal canyons in southern California.

Dense understory brush is another. Large brushy areas with few or no open, brush-free areas are bad for turkeys and not so good for most other wildlife, either. Private landowners need to learn to use *appropriately-timed* burns to make their woodlands better for both wildlife and timber production.

Fertilizing pastures and croplands with poultry litter. Most if not all poultry houses use rice or wheat hulls, sawdust, peanut shells or similar organic materials for floor litter. Combined with the semi-liquid stuff it's there to absorb, it's about as rich a fertilizer as you'll find. After a batch of birds is raised and sent to market, it has to be disposed of. Many poultry growers spread the spent litter on their fields. Some also sell the stuff or give it away by the pickup load to gardeners or neighbors.

It doesn't take a systems analyst to see the potential danger here. Sure enough, there are more than a few documented cases where poultry litter has introduced disease into wild turkey populations, resulting in significant localized population declines. The solution is both simple and difficult: quit spreading poultry litter. There are many other options besides scooping it up and spreading it on hayfields. Look it up; I did.

Baiting. Call it baiting or feeding, potato potahto. It's not a good idea with deer, wild turkeys and other species either. Most baiting/feeding uses corn, and most so-called "deer corn" is either uncleaned, or is corn that has failed to pass tests for human consumption.

Uncleaned corn often contains cockleburs and other undesirable plant seeds. Nuff said there, but have you heard of aflatoxins? We don't need to get into a chemistry lesson here, but this is a group of poisonous carcinogens that are produced by some molds, and they're commonly found in stored grains such as – you guessed it – corn. Aflatoxins are tough on pretty much everything that walks, crawls or flies through the air, so that's one huge reason not to feed corn to wildlife.

Another reason: putting up feeders causes an artificial situation where wild critters come into much closer and more prolonged contact. Just as contagious human diseases are spread more easily in crowds, so are wildlife diseases.

Also, feeders create easy hunting conditions for predators, just as they do for hunters. All a coyote or bobcat needs to do is lie in wait until something tasty shows up. And don't think for a minute that coyotes and cats aren't smart enough to figure it out.

Skilled but unlawful and/or unethical hunters. Like it or not, we turkey hunters are often our own worst enemies. There are thugs and outlaws among us. You know some of these folks and I do, too. They hunt before and after the season, they hunt over bait, they shoot turkeys off the roost, they don't tag and register their kills, they trespass. Name it, and if it can help them deaden another turkey they'll give it a whirl.

The problem here is twofold. Sadly, many of these outlaws are also skilled turkey hunters, so they're pretty efficient in their outlawing. Secondly, even though their illegal activities may be common knowledge, nobody wants to be labeled a snitch so nobody reports them. And very few of us even go as far as to exert peer pressure on the outlaws, even though their activities are hurting us all.

We need to stop feeling that way. You'd turn in a bank robber or a car thief, wouldn't you? So drop the dime on poachers, and also don't be afraid to tell them you think they're despicable. I've done both and will continue to do so. It feels pretty damn good, actually.

The media

Shame on you, Outdoor Channel, Pursuit Channel and all the other networks that air those watch-me-kill-stuff shows one after another. Shame on you, the TV shows themselves, because most of them generally feature fully-camo'ed "hunters" sitting in Double Bull blinds or perched in trees, watching decoys and/or food plots for a deer or turkey to show up. Sorry, but that ain't hunting. Shame on you, hunters who regularly publish look-at-me YouTube videos of successful outings. Shame on you, body-counters who splash your dead-critter pictures all over social media, usually with yourself in the picture striking a heroic pose.

And yes, shame on me and all my brothers and sisters in the outdoor promotion industry – writers, photographers, artists, radio people, seminar givers, pro-staffers, TV producers, whatever – for promoting the idea that hunting in general and turkey hunting in particular is somehow glamorous and sexy, when the truth is, it's damned hard work and frustrating besides. The NWTF has played a big role in this as well, by getting many, many more people interested in turkey hunting without bothering to explain to them what they're really getting into.

Collectively, we've created a monster. I know there's strength in numbers, and I know newcomers are necessary for turkey hunting's survival. I also know the incoming turkey hunter who makes his first hunt next spring has as much right to be out there as the white-bearded old goat who's been chasing them for half a century.

But I know this, too: there are some six million turkeys in the United States, and there are more than three million turkey hunters out there after them. That kind of arithmetic simply doesn't work. With all the other problems besetting turkey populations today, stirring a huge amount of hunting pressure into the mix isn't helping, no matter how much we tell ourselves hunter mortality is not additive but compensatory, and no matter how much we tell ourselves there's strength in numbers.

This current situation is not sustainable. We have to make some changes.

* * *

Epilogue

So. Where *do* we go from here? Well, here's the unsolicited opinion of one of those white-bearded old goats, one who has spent 1,237 days on the hunt (no fooling, 1,237 – I just went through my log books and added it up): I think we need to – scratch that; we *must* – get better at educating folks that turkey hunting is about much more than killing a turkey and posting it on Facegram or Instabook. This is not about body counts.

Granted, a turkey hunt without the possibility of a kill would be about as much fun as prepping for a colonoscopy, but still. There's way more to it than pulling the trigger, and we *must* start communicating that.

That's easy for me to say, I know. I've done my share of killing in those 1,237 days. Given that much time, even the most inept hunter would stumble over a few suicidal turkeys. But if every other turkey hunter in America had also spent more than 3 years on the hunt, this situation would likely be far worse than it already is.

So like it or not, I've been an actual, physical part of the problem, not to mention having helped fan the flames by writing more than a thousand stories about turkey hunting and two (now three) books on the subject. Some of that verbiage, if for no other reason than sheer volume, has to have encouraged somebody, somewhere, to give turkey hunting a try.

Self-professed trout bum John Gierach says in his latest book, *Dumb Luck and the Kindness of Strangers:* "We measure ourselves by our successes if only because our many failures don't make for much of a story." I'm not sure I buy that. My conceit is, the stories of failure in this book (also in *Turkey Hunting Digest* and the first *Bad Birds*, both available on eBay, hint, hint) go a long way toward disproving that. Some of the best memories I have are those days when I got clobbered.

I still love to shoot turkeys. If I claimed otherwise I'd be lying and you'd know it. But these days I'm a little more inclined toward charity. Instead of trying to kill gobblers in double figures every spring,

Bad Birds 2

I find myself letting one walk now and then.

Take last spring, for example. I tagged one gobbler. One. Granted, there were a couple epic failures, during one of which I missed the same turkey twice on the same morning, with an hour between misses. But mostly, my low tally was because I didn't shoot at every

My life has been enriched by the pursuit of wild turkeys.

turkey I might have killed. Shooting through brush? I held off on that, not once but twice. Stretching the gun barrel a little? Five times on that one. Flying turkey? Three times. Running turkey? Once.

One dead turkey. And I still had a very enjoyable season.

* * *

That's what we all need to do, I think. Pull back on the reins a little bit. Don't slack off on your hunting efforts; I'm not suggesting that at all. But look in the mirror and admit that you're part of the problem. I'm part of it, too, but I'm trying to fix that.

Try to discipline yourself to pass up those iffy shots. Pattern your shotgun until you know the range where it loses punch or pattern, then resist those *when-there's-lead-in-the-air-there's-hope-in-the-heart* shots out there on the ragged edge. Likewise, don't shoot if there's brush in the way. Don't body-shoot turkeys. Don't shoot them flying, either, because you're mostly shooting them in the ass and you're not likely to kill one that way. More than likely, they'll get away crippled.

Just those four things would vastly reduce the number of cripples that escape, only to die and be wasted. Turkeys are much too valuable for that, and we can do a lot to prevent it merely by exercising a little restraint. Letting a turkey walk feels awful, but watching a cripple fly off with a leg dangling feels awfuller.

But we can all do more. Another thing is to individually educate our fellow turkey hunters. If you know somebody who's struggling, or who isn't showing the proper respect to the bird, to other hunters or to turkey hunting itself, then dummy, do something about it. Make a friend, not an enemy. Have a quiet, nonconfrontational conversation about doing things right. Better yet, invite them to go hunting and teach by example. I'd much rather share the woods with a hunter who knows proper etiquette than one who doesn't. Wouldn't you?

One more thing we can do as individuals is give something

back. Take part in wildlife agency surveys. Volunteer for habitat improvement projects. Put in a food plot or two if you have land for it, or help a friend with his. Simply get off your butt during the off season and *go do something*. You'll feel better about yourself, and you'll be doing your part to reverse this trend.

And make no mistake, we can reverse it. Bad weather and poor hatches are largely beyond our control, but we have a lot of influence in other areas if we'll just use it. We've brought turkeys back once already, and they were a lot farther down the toilet then than now. For the past 120-odd years, since we woke up, hunters have always been wildlife's greatest ally.

That hasn't changed. Let's all roll up our sleeves and make it happen again.

* * *

Two generations of humans have reached adulthood on Planet Earth since I looked down the gyrating barrel of a borrowed shotgun at what was about to become my first turkey. (Two days after I pulled the trigger on that gobbler, John Warnock Hinckley, Jr. pulled another trigger on President Ronald Reagan. That's how long ago we're talking about here.)

But that shocking assassination attempt was still 48 hours in the future as this pencil-bearded two-year-old approached. I sat there trembling, my pulse hammering so hard it made my eyeballs hurt. Thank God the turkey came in fast or I think my heart might have exploded.

The late Robert Steinmetz sat beside me and called in that first gobbler. I've told the story before and won't bore you with it here, but for the sake of full disclosure I admit I had little to do with the event. My role was to hyperventilate, tremble and quake, shoot the gobbler in the head, run whooping out there to claim it, then go behind a bush and puke up my breakfast.

Robert engineered the whole affair, taking me hunting that day after spending several hours the previous week coaching me, educating me. How to sit as a turkey approached. How to get my knees up and rest my elbows on them. How to keep still when necessary, and how to know when it was okay to move the gun. What part of the turkey to aim at. All that stuff turkey hunters must know that I didn't.

In the process of teaching me those first-grader basics, Robert molded an eager but clueless hunk of protoplasm into an eager hunk of protoplasm with a vague idea of what to do.

Robert is gone now, God rest him, and I've spent a lifetime trying to build on that foundation he laid under me. I've learned some things. And even now, after all this time, when I'm standing there in the growing dawn and waiting for the first gobble, I'm still that eager hunk of protoplasm that lost its cookies behind a bush.

But in truth, I still have only a vague idea of what to do when I hear it.

Bad Birds 2

This photo of a moth-eaten mounted gobbler has absolutely nothing to do with any of the gloomy content of the preceding epilogue. It is simply the author's lame attempt to end this book on a light note. Have you ever seen anything uglier?

On the other hand, have you ever seen anything prettier?

www.ingramcontent.com/pod-product-compliance
Lightning Source LLC
Chambersburg PA
CBHW071806080526
44589CB00012B/708